Ask
Dale Murphy

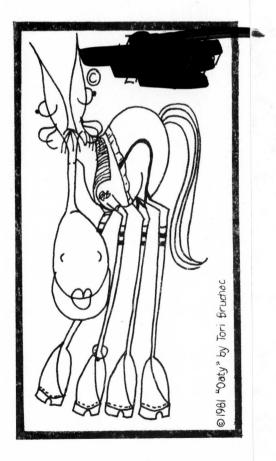

© 1981 "Oaty" by Tori Bruchac

Dale Murphy being congratulated by his teammates after a ninth-inning game-winning homer.—*W. A. Bridges, Jr., Atlanta Journal & Constitution*

Ask
Dale Murphy

By Dale Murphy
with Curtis Patton

Introduction by Furman Bisher

Chapel Hill and Dallas
An Algonquin/Taylor Book
1987

To Nancy,
To Chad, Shawn, Travis, and Tyson,
and to our parents.
           D.M.
           C.P.

This Algonquin/Taylor book is a joint publication of
Algonquin Books of Chapel Hill
Post Office Box 2225,
Chapel Hill, North Carolina 27515-2225
and
Taylor Publishing Company
1550 West Mockingbird Avenue
Dallas, Texas 75235
and is distributed by Taylor Publishing Company.
In their original form most of the questions and answers included in *Ask
Dale Murphy* appeared first in the pages of the *Atlanta Journal &
Constitution*.

Library of Congress Cataloging-in-Publication Data
Murphy, Dale, 1956–
   Ask Dale Murphy.

   1. Murphy, Dale, 1956–   .   2. Baseball players—
United States—Biography.   3. Baseball—United States.
I. Patton, Curtis, 1946–   .   II. Title.
GV865.M79A3   1987   796.357′092′4 [B]   86-28677
ISBN 0-912967-59-8

Contents

Introduction, *Furman Bisher*   vii

Preface   ix

I.   Breaking into Baseball   3

II.   Hitting a Baseball   25

III. The Defensive Game   45

IV. It's How You Play the Game: The Right Attitude   57

V.   Life in the Major Leagues   77

VI. Family and Future Plans   91

Introduction

By Furman Bisher

It had first entered my mind that I should begin this introduction with this thought: "If I had a son, it would please me enormously if he were like Dale Murphy."

Then I caught myself. I already had three sons, with whom I am very pleased.

All right, then, if I had a fourth son, I would like him to be like Dale Murphy.

Having bridged that crevasse, I move ahead to state that such a thought represents no risk in any form. I can be positively, absolutely assured that he will not embarrass us all by being picked up for causing a disturbance in some shady tavern, nor for cursing his manager. His mission in life is being himself, and being Dale Murphy may have led many a boy child to say, "If I had a second daddy, I wish he could be like Dale Murphy."

There are four Murphys who live in that happy circumstance, and that is to confirm that Dale Murphy knows young people. While he is a traveling man, due to the demands of the business in which he is engaged, he reserves time for his own brood. He is one who would view disdainfully a father who doesn't know his own children.

"Ask Dale Murphy" began as a newspaper column in *The Journal & Constitution*. The root source was my desk, and I would be shamefully remiss if I did not confess that the inspiration came from something I had seen of similar work by Pat McInally in the Cincinnati area, while he played for the Bengals of the National Football League. Dale fit the mould perfectly, and has since Day One, with the counsel of his sidekick, as they say in the West, Curtis Patton.

It will be quite discernible that Dale does not speak to you from a pedestal. He is no lecturer mounted on a soapbox. He engages in exchange, your ideas in question form, then his ideas in response in which he comes across as one mortal to another.

The humility you see here is not practiced, it is real. As in the following: "Sometimes when I swing and miss, I start to wonder if I can hit anything."

This is the same man who has twice been elected the Most Valuable Player in the National League; whose career is only ten years long, but whose record already requires one full page in the *Baseball Register.*

Dale Murphy is as sensitive a man in expressing himself as he is adroit in centerfield. As perfect as he may seem, he makes no attempt to gloss over his flaws, his glitches and his frustrations. Notice that he went to bat over 100 times before he was able to hit his first home run in the big leagues.

He has known the despair that comes with failure. Notice the other positions listed by his name before he finally became a fulltime outfielder. The Atlanta Braves signed him to be a catcher, but he was a homesick lad who failed to hit well and developed a problem simply in returning the ball to the pitcher. He was tried at first base, a natural target, it seemed, six feet, four inches tall and all that wingspan. Bobby Cox, the manager, saw him floundering there and settled upon the position of centerfield, which began as an experiment and evolved as a stroke of genius. Murphy was like a colt unhaltered. He was free of the constrictions of the plate and the infield, and given all that space in which to roam, he was allowed to exercise his swift feet and strong arm. He caught hold of a passing star, and since the season of 1981, there has been no more consistent player in the National League.

Equally consistent is his demeanor and his personality. Seldom does he speak a discouraging word. Rarely is he without a smile on his face. He can be accommodating, sometimes to his own detriment. He draws the line, though, at the invasion of his clubhouse privacy by female members of the media, for what manner of man chooses to have himself observed in his toiletry by a member of the opposite sex to whom he hasn't been introduced?

On the other hand, I arrived at the stadium one afternoon and located him out by the Braves dugout signing autographs and visiting with a cluster of young people he'd promised to meet there. At the same time he was worrying about the whereabouts of a photographer who had asked to meet him. These were not easy times for him, for the Braves were not having a good season, nor was he.

What Dale Murphy contributes to American sports goes well beyond the mere accumulation of numbers beside his name. He bespeaks a kind of character too often found lacking in men who are stars. They discover stardom, they come to ignore the blessing that provided them the way.

The goodness and the warmth of Dale Murphy's nature sometimes causes puzzled scrutiny in the passing journalist. How many times has it been that I've had a visiting writer quietly approach and ask, "Look, is this man for real? Is he what I think I'm seeing? It just seems he's too good to be true."

What you see is true. What you read is from the heart. You go to a doctor for medical advice. You see the dentist when your teeth need care. You visit the barber when your hair gets too long.

Now, "Ask Dale Murphy." You'll get a straight answer with a touch of humor. It comes to you right out of centerfield.

Preface

Baseball is a game for the young. Maybe the title of Roger Kahn's book, *The Boys of Summer,* is the best way to think about it. I'm one of a very few fortunate people who are able to keep playing it past their youth. But it hasn't been very long since I was only one of hundreds of thousands of little leaguers, playing baseball with my friends and dreaming, like them, of making it to the major leagues. That my dream happened to come true isn't the important thing. It's the dream that matters, because the dream is part of the fun of being young and playing ball.

Now that I've turned thirty and have youngsters of my own, it won't be long before they'll be having the same dream and, I hope, the same kind of fun I had playing baseball. Whether, like me, any of my boys become professional athletes, or whether some other dream happens to come true for them instead, no one can say. What I want them to do is to have fun being young and playing ball or whatever they'd like to have fun doing. Nancy and I certainly don't intend to push them in the direction of baseball. What they do will be up to them, and what as parents we want is for them to grow up to be good people and good citizens.

Young people today have all kinds of opportunities, and often they're subjected to all kinds of pressures and temptations. What worries me sometimes is that with the best of intentions their parents and their little league coaches push them too hard to succeed, so that what ought to be the fun of being young and playing games is taken from them. Too often adults try to relive their own younger days and work out their adult competitive desires through young people. When that happens, playing baseball, or any other sport, ceases to be a game. The young people playing it, and who should be having fun, become an excuse for adults to compete against each other. Fortunately it isn't usually that way. I have nothing but respect and admiration for most of the tens of thousands of parents, coaches and other adults who devote their time and energy to young people, and who don't lose sight of the fact that what they're doing is helping young people to play, and to have fun doing it. I often wonder where I would be without the dedicated work of my parents—and all those other parents and coaches—when I was growing up. To all of them I am most grateful.

When a few years ago the *Atlanta Journal & Constitution* invited me to write a regular feature every week, answering questions about the game of baseball and related things sent in by young people, I thought it would be an opportunity to encourage and help them to enjoy playing ball. My friend Curtis Patton agreed to work with me on it. What Curtis and I wanted to do was to help them by giving advice about how the game is played and also how to have fun doing it.

Many of the questions we've answered are technical. Some are about my own life as a professional ball player. Others are about their attitude, their relations with parents and coaches. We've tried to answer the questions honestly, and to take the problems they bring up seriously.

For this book we have selected some of the questions we've been asked, and our answers to them, that we think will be interesting to young people not only in the circulation area of the *Atlanta Journal & Constitution* but wherever young people play and watch baseball. We hope that readers everywhere will enjoy it. If some of those readers are adults who played the summer game when they were young and who still watch it, so much the better.

We should like to thank Furman Bisher, sports editor of the *Atlanta Journal & Constitution*, for his role in making the newspaper column possible and for his willingness to write an introduction to this book. For help in providing some of the photographs we are grateful to the *Atlanta Journal & Constitution*, and the Atlanta Braves.

Our thanks, also, go to my agent, Bruce Church.

Dale Murphy

Atlanta, Georgia
September 30, 1986

Ask
Dale Murphy

The West Hills Home little leaguers, Portland, Oregon, 1960; *Seated*, Dale Murphy, batboy; *top right*, his father—Charles Murphy, coach; *top left*, Ken Robinson, other coach. *Below*, Dale as a rookie professional with Kingsport, Tennessee, in the Appalachian League in 1974.

I. Breaking Into Baseball

What age did you start playing baseball and who helped you the most to be a major-league ballplayer?—*Brad Kjera, 8*

I started playing organized baseball at age eight.

It's kind of hard putting a finger on who exactly has been the most helpful. There have been so many—starting with Mom and Dad, who gave me the opportunity to be involved in athletics.

And then, there is the baseball program at Woodrow Wilson High School in Portland, Oregon, under my high school coach, Jack Dunn. I still feel that he's one of the most knowledgeable men as far as knowing baseball and teaching baseball to kids or anyone. That background really helped me.

I also think about our summer program in American Legion baseball. If the sponsor is willing to spend some money on your team, you can get to play in a lot of games. Marion Reneau was the man who sponsored us, paid for a lot of trips and gave us a lot of exposure. It gave me the opportunity to be seen by major-league scouts, which was very helpful.

Then I got drafted by the Atlanta Braves, and the help still continues. I had some people who encouraged me and stuck by me—such as the late Bill Lucas, and Paul Snyder, who's still with the Braves—who helped me when things weren't going well in my minor-league career.

So it has been a varied group of people who have really helped me to make it. And there are many people to thank.

When you were little, did you ever think you would become a famous baseball player?—*Amy Warren, 12*

That's nice of you to say that. I don't feel like a famous baseball player. I don't really feel any different than when I was playing as a kid. I just feel like I'm doing something I did in high school.

I never really thought that I wanted to play professional baseball as a kid, though it was definitely a dream of mine. And I gave it serious thought when I was older.

But I never thought about being famous. As a kid, baseball just looked like a lot of fun, and I never thought about a lot of people watching. Of course, as I got older I recognized that nearly everyone enjoys watching professional sports.

I realize that if a guy plays in the major leagues, he does get a lot of publicity. We play on TV a lot, and we get notoriety for being baseball players. It's something a player kind of enjoys, but I don't feel any different, except that people ask me for my autograph a little bit more than they did in high school. I still feel the same.

Did your father influence you to play baseball?
—Dawn Atkinson, 11

I don't really feel that he influenced me in that decision. In fact, when it came down to my decision as to whether to go to college or to sign a professional contract with the Braves, my mother and father basically told me: "It will be your decision, Dale, and we will support you either way you decide."

But as a youngster, I think the great thing my dad provided me was himself—to play catch with me once in a while. It wasn't necessarily baseball. It might have been shooting baskets or throwing the football. I don't think I was steered into any sort of profession. He just gave me the opportunity to play Little League.

I think the main thing about being involved in amateur athletics is that it gives you the opportunity to grow and to learn how to compete, how to win and how to lose.

I'm thankful that my dad gave me the opportunity if I wanted to play. And if I didn't want to play baseball, I think he would have supported me as well.

I'm thankful for my dad, and my mom as well, for putting up with all the broken windows from us playing catch.

My dad would often come home from work tired, but he would go out there and play catch with me. I know that many times, probably, he didn't want to, but that's one thing I appreciate about him.

What were your favorite baseball teams when you were growing up? Why were they?—*Russell Blake, 12*

I guess the reason most people pick a team is because they live, or have lived, near the team at one time.

When I was nine years old, my father was transferred to San Francisco, so we moved from Portland, Oregon, to near San Francisco. That was the first chance I got to see a major-league game, and it was the San Francisco Giants playing.

That's when I first started following baseball. I can remember a few times I even kept score. My dad taught me how, and I thought it was a neat thing that I could actually keep score on a little score pad. So I would listen on the radio and keep score.

The Giants were the first team I followed and really pulled for, but I also liked to watch the Oakland A's. I was in the area when Catfish Hunter pitched a perfect game, and I enjoyed following the Athletics as well as the Giants.

Who was your hero when you were a kid? Who is your hero now?—*Jay Sanders, 9*

When I was a youngster watching the San Francisco Giants, I loved Willie Mays. He was exciting and just a great ballplayer.

When I got into high school, I started to catch, so I followed Johnny Bench. I tried to imitate him every time I caught. Every time I was the catcher, I tried to remember how Johnny Bench would do it.

Now as a professional baseball player, my perspective has changed. My real heroes now are my parents, for what they have done for me and for what they are doing for me. I also look at the people who are working hard and trying to make a good living for their families. My heroes, too, are the people who put their families first.

If you liked the A's and the Giants, why did you go to the Braves?—*John Hubbard, 10*

At one time, there was no draft in baseball. Players out of high school or college were free agents and could talk to any team they chose. They basically could sign with any team they wanted to, or whoever gave them the most money.

Beginning in 1965 players were drafted by various teams and could negotiate only with that team. I was drafted in the first round of the 1974 draft by the Braves, so my only option was to negotiate with the Braves, and I signed a contract. I really didn't have a choice where I wanted to go.

But the first goal of any young player is just to make it to the major leagues. That's the most important thing. I still feel that way now. As a youngster, I'm sure I had some teams I kind of wanted to play for, but it wasn't something I had a choice in.

I'm thankful, however, that I've had the opportunity to play in the major leagues and to work with the fine people in the Atlanta organization.

Are you a natural lefthander? If so, why do you bat and throw right-handed? And how did you learn to bat right-handed?—*Melissa Phillips, 15*

For some reason, I first started writing left-handed and eating with my left hand, but when I picked up a baseball to throw it I used my right hand.

I feel like I'm naturally left-handed. But I don't know why I started using my right hand in baseball. I've never done it any other way. I'm just guessing, but maybe it was because my dad was throwing right-handed to me. He's a natural righthander, and I just saw him throwing it and thought that I was supposed to throw it the same way.

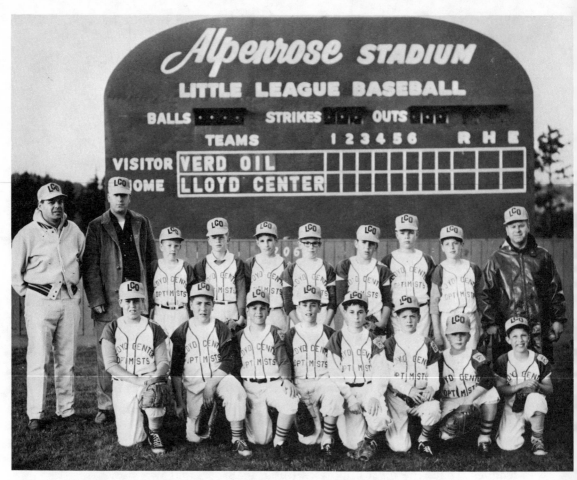

Dale, age 9, is third from right, front row, in this photograph of the Lloyd Center Optimists in 1965.

I started hitting right-handed as well and wasn't really taught anything about how to hit left-handed. I remember seeing left-handed hitters at bat as a youngster and thinking that's pretty odd. Nearly everyone batted right-handed.

But basically, the best bet for a baseball player is to be a right-handed thrower and a left-handed hitter or a switch hitter. Switch hitting obviously has its advantages, but being a left-handed hitter has advantages as well because there are more right-handed pitchers. You get a better look at things.

What was your batting average in high school? Did you hit many home runs?—*Greg Bodager, 8*

I don't remember. I know my batting average my senior year was .432, but I don't think I hit many home runs. I never hit many homers until I was 21 years old, when I was at Richmond, Virginia, in Triple A ball. I hit 21 home runs in 1977 with Richmond.

I wasn't really a power hitter in those days. Most pitchers then threw fastballs, not sliders or curves. We only played 15–20 games, and it was rainy in Portland, Oregon, so we just played games when we could. And we played some games at places where there were no fences.

What made you decide on baseball as a career?

—Tara Lewis, 11

I didn't really think about it as a career until the Atlanta Braves drafted me and gave me a chance to play major league baseball in 1974.

Baseball was the only high school sport I really excelled in. I was going to go to Arizona State and play baseball there, but I never considered pro baseball seriously until the Braves asked me. I was going to give it about five years of minor league ball. If I didn't make it to the majors by then, I was going to re-evaluate my chances and maybe go on to something else.

What does it take to make it as a pro ballplayer? Do they look at speed, batting and fielding statistics?—*Steve Oldham, 17*

The main things a team looks for now are hitting, defensive ability and speed. The last few years, the game has been restructured around speed, and scouts make that a top priority.

In a pitcher, scouts look at how hard he throws more than his control. (They believe a pitcher, with maturity, can improve on control.)

In an infielder-outfielder, scouts look at arm strength, speed, defense and, of course, hitting.

Dale's youthful idol, Willie Mays of the San Francisco Giants; and Dale with his parents, Charles and Betty Murphy, at Candlestick Park in San Francisco in 1986.—*Mays photo courtesy Atlanta Journal & Constitution*

In a catcher, scouts look more at defensive abilities.

But there are other things to consider: Baseball sense, desire and ability to work hard. Two examples come to mind: Shortstop Larry Bowa, who played for the Philadelphia Phillies and the Chicago Cubs for sixteen seasons, and Pete Rose, who broke Ty Cobb's record for the most base hits ever.

Bowa had trouble making his high school team at first, and the scouting report on Rose—at the peak of his career—was that he had an average arm and average speed. But both made the best of their ability, and both had the desire to make it.

It's not always the guys with the most talent who succeed. Many picked in the first round of the baseball draft never make it, but others chosen very late do make it. So the most important thing scouts are looking for is a person who's willing to pay the price.

I am interested in playing in the majors like you. Can you tell me some of the things I need to do to build up a strong arm?— *Erick Pennington, 10*

I think some people are just born with it. Some people with the skinniest arms throw really hard.

I wouldn't be too concerned about your arm strength right now. When you get into high school and get a little older, you'll be strong enough to work out with weights to strengthen your arms.

Right now, make sure you don't hurt your arm before you get to high school. So take care of your arm and don't throw until it hurts every day. Take a few days. If it hurts, don't throw. Your body is trying to tell you something, so take care of it. As you get bigger your arm strength will improve.

One drill I would recommend, after warming up, is where you play catch at long distances, because your arm muscles need to be conditioned for throwing a long distance, the 60 or 90 feet in the infield. Don't throw it hard, just throw it with the proper form, directly overhand, and basically throw fly balls to each other.

When I grow up, I want to play professional baseball. My mom says I should go to college anyway. Do I have to go to college?— *Jay Sanders, 9*

Do you think a college education is necessary in order to play baseball?— *Melissa Mobley, 10*

A college education isn't necessary to play baseball, but it helps.

The way professional baseball works now is that you don't have to go to college to play ball. You can sign right out of high school and

At the Murphy grandparents' farm in Brady, Nebraska, in 1967, when Dale was 11.

go to a minor league professional team. Football and basketball have the college teams, which are more or less their minor league systems. They draft their players after they finish their college careers—or sooner.

Technically, there is an opportunity for some high school players after they are graduated to play professional baseball. Some high school graduates go to a junior college for a couple of years and get drafted. You can also get drafted at any time during junior college. Right now the rules say if you go to a four-year college, you have to wait until you are 21 or after your junior year before you can be drafted.

The thing that I would encourage you to do first of all is to evaluate yourself and your goals in life when you get to the end of your high school years. You have to look at things realistically. You have to rely on something else if your aspiration to play in the major leagues is cut short, possibly by injury or if you don't make the team. If things don't work out and you were drafted high enough, you can fall back on your signing bonus—if it's enough money—to compensate for your missing a college education.

An education is so important, and you need to evaluate that. There are many major league players who have gone two or three years to a junior college or major university. And if things didn't work out in baseball, they had part of their education fulfilled.

It's hard to make up for lost time in getting an education. But you definitely can do both—play ball and get an education.

I have played baseball for eight years, and it has always been my favorite sport. Right now I am seventeen years old and I am interested in becoming a coach. What can I do now to prepare for becoming a high school or college baseball coach?— *Brad Woodall*

Obviously, as much baseball playing experience as you can get is important. I would recommend you just study the game as much as you can and play the game so you can get some first-hand experience like you already have.

The next thing is to pick the school you want to go to, and maybe you'll get the chance at some student assistant coaching. You can get some experience that way.

I would suggest that you write college coaches right now and get all the information you can on how they got their jobs and what background they have: education and baseball experience.

There are also many clinics and college coaches' conventions where you can meet a lot of people and tell them of your interests. But get a good education first and accept every opportunity to play the game.

Dale with the Greenwood, South Carolina, Braves in 1975; and with his teammate Barry Bonnell on the Savannah, Georgia, Braves in 1976. Barry also made it to the majors playing with Atlanta, Toronto, and Seattle.

I've always thought it would be fun to coach college or high school-age kids, because they are not at the point in professional baseball where they know so much that they are hard to teach.

What advice would you give to a young person who really wants to be a ball player?—*Sherry McCullough, 12*

I think the best advice I could give to you is to enjoy the game of baseball right now—at a young age—and other activities in life as well. You may grow up thinking, "Hey, I wish I could do something else."

When you're young, you need to experience a lot of things. You might find you like some things better than others. You don't really need to be thinking about baseball as a career at a young age. Things might not work out, so it's best to get a good education, a good schooling, and to experience a lot of other sports and activities.

The thing to do now in baseball is just to make sure you are in shape, healthy and practice the basic skills—hitting, running, throwing, whatever you can. But don't let baseball dominate your life at a young age when there are other things you could experience.

I would like to know how to improve my game: hitting, catching and throwing.—*Kevin Pace, 13*

You have to practice. The guys who make it practice the hardest. Once you get into the game, it's really just a result of practicing and working at your job, at your particular sport.

Games aren't always won on the field. Sometimes they are won during the practice session, or spring training, or during the off-season by getting yourself in good shape. You are really preparing yourself for the game.

So just do a number of things to work on those skills. Two guys can play a game. You can get against a wall and have someone pitch tennis balls to you, or some kind of ball. Or play stickball and have the strike zone painted on the wall somewhere. You pitch to your friend and try to get him out and then switch roles.

I used to play a game called ground ball where we would get 30, 40 or 50 feet away from each other and throw ground balls and try to get the other guy to miss them. If I caught it, it was an out, and we played until I made three outs, then we switched.

Playing games such as these will improve your skills. But it takes a lot of practice. And you can make it fun. Don't make practice something that is not enjoyable, and don't do it alone. If it seems like a chore, and you don't like it, don't go out and torture yourself. But if you like baseball, go out and play and have fun.

Top, the "Wilson High Monster" of 1974, with Dale below, carrying Jeff Dunn on his shoulders; right, Dale and his sister Susan, now Mrs. Doug Moss, at Christmastime, 1974; below, Dale's high school graduation photo, 1974.

I would like to know how to overcome ball-shyness. I play softball, and once in a while I close my eyes when I'm trying to catch or field. It's not really that bad, but it hinders my game. Do you have any suggestions on how to cure this problem?—*Julie Gail Lanier, 13*

All of us who have played major-league baseball have gone through times when we were learning to play when we were afraid of the ball. I think every person goes through that. The best thing you can do is keep practicing. Work at keeping your eyes open.

There's nothing wrong with having that fear at times, because you're human, and that's a natural thing to have. The only way you can overcome that is to keep practicing. You'll eventually overcome the problem, because you'll have the confidence in yourself, and you'll be able to catch the ball.

It's like riding a bike. At first you're really wobbly, and you need someone to hold you up. Then one day you just get on the bike, and you're able to ride. You've figured out the coordination and balance to keep the bike moving. And it all comes from practice.

My father says in most cases it's better to throw overhand. Sometimes I throw sidearm. Today I noticed you threw sidearm. Which way is better?—*William Russell, 6*

There's no question that when you're learning to throw a baseball it's best to throw overhand. There is backspin on the ball when you throw overhand and sidespin when you throw sidearm. You actually get a truer flight of the ball—and better control—by throwing overhand. If you look carefully, you will notice the ball moves differently when it's thrown sidearm.

As you get older and into high school, and your skills improve, you can experiment throwing sidearm. But right now, practice throwing the ball overhand as much as you can.

A lot of professional players throw the ball both ways. But we have practiced for years. Some pitchers also throw it both ways. A sidearm pitch is not thrown as hard as an overhand pitch. But because of the movement of the ball, a sidearm pitch is harder to hit.

I play Little League baseball. I am trying to learn to pitch. Should I learn to throw a curve ball? My dad said I'm too young to throw a curve ball. What do you think?

—*Chris Allen, 8*

I don't have a medical background or anything medically to back up my opinion, but I have to go along with your father on this.

There is a division of opinion about learning to throw a curve. One opinion is that if you are taught to throw a curve ball properly, it won't hurt you at any age. The key there is "taught properly."

But personally, I think you should wait until your bones and muscles develop a little bit more. I don't know if I can say there is an exact age when you can learn how to throw a curve ball. But I think I would give it a few more years anyway.

Just throwing the fastball is hard enough on your arm without putting the extra pressure on your elbow from throwing a curve. I would wait.

I have a dear grandson, a little over three years old and small for his age, who weighs about thirty pounds. He has been given a teeball bat and two regular hard baseballs. I think he is too little and too young to play teeball. What is your opinion?—*J.B. Handley*

He is not too young to learn how to play ball and develop hand-eye coordination. It's always good for a kid to learn how to catch and to throw a ball.

I always worked with my kids very early, so that they would learn how to manipulate their hands. But a child definitely has to be careful with a hard baseball at three years of age. Even my oldest son, Chad, gets a bat sometimes that's too heavy for him.

Starting him out at age three with teeball is not going to determine whether he will be a major-league ballplayer. It's not going to give him an advantage. But goofing around with a plastic Whiffle ball and bat is probably the best for your grandson right now. He can learn coordination and balance and how to use his arms and hands. I think that's what's important for a child that age. And he can develop with any kind of ball, large or small. But a soft, bouncy one is best for him.

I play Little League, and I'm the only girl on the team, besides Chrissy. When I strike out, sometimes the boys give me a hard time. What should I do?—*Patty George, 10*

That's really a hard part of the game. It's unfortunate that your teammates would give you a bad time like that.

Sometimes when I strike out—in Chicago, for instance—I have plenty of people in the stands reminding me of what I did my last time at bat. That's to be expected. That's some people's way of having fun, I guess—to give you a bad time when you don't do well.

I'm really sorry to hear that the people who would give you a bad time are on your own team. If I strike out, I may hear a few yells from the stands, but the guys on my team encourage me, saying, "Don't worry about it, Murph, you'll get them the next time," or something like that.

The best thing I can tell you is to do your best to ignore the bad times these people are giving you. When someone strikes out, just go up and encourage them to get them the next time.

My advice to you—and this will probably be pretty hard for you—is to encourage those who would discourage you. Eventually that will change their outlook.

How do you make a good play when you are short as four foot or three foot something?—*Shane McGill, 11*

It's been proven over and over again that height has little to do with athletic ability. Sometimes it helps, but it definitely isn't always the margin for making or not making the good play.

In basketball it seems to help to be taller than average, but there have been many players who have proven that physical size is not as important as attitude and desire.

Being tall isn't the main ingredient for being a good player. Doug Flutie, quarterback in the NFL, is not as tall as most quarterbacks playing professional football, and there have been—and are now—baseball and basketball players who have proven that size doesn't count. So you may not be as tall and as strong as other people, but it doesn't mean that you can't work harder and think better and be a little quicker than taller people.

You'll notice that most shortstops and second basemen aren't as tall as outfielders and first basemen because they need to be quicker. Height is an advantage, but quickness is another.

Do you think it is better to focus on just one sport or to enjoy different sports?—*Leland Barrow, 6*

I definitely think you need to experience as many sports as you would like.

At your age it's important to find out what you like, and maybe in high school you could concentrate a little heavier on one sport. Even then, you could still play several sports and see what you like. And if you're able to continue in athletics in college, you'll be able to specialize your talents.

But now it's important to participate in sports you would like to try and learn as much as you can about each sport. That's why you take different subjects in school: To get a broad base of knowledge so you'll know what you want to be when you grow up.

You'll discover that as you grow your feelings about different sports will change. When I was in the seventh and eighth grade, I was

Dale Murphy as a little league pitcher, Moraga, California, in 1967.

probably leaning a lot more toward basketball. I really enjoyed basketball, football and baseball. But when I got into high school, I started leaning toward baseball.

And I'm thankful I'm still doing something that I enjoyed as a youngster. And when you find out what you would like to do, maybe someday it could be your job, too.

Did you have to do your school work before you played baseball?—*Melissa Hunley, 8*

I would like to know how you can practice when you have a bunch of homework and it's going to take so long that you're late for the practice.—*Justin Cawthon, 8*

I know that baseball is an important part of your life right now, but I would have to remind you that it's most important to get your school work done and make sure baseball doesn't interfere. There isn't any reason you can't do both.

I've played baseball since I was eight years old, and there's no reason why you can't participate in athletics and also go to school. As you get older and go into high school, you will have even more homework and things to do.

There is time to do both. It's important that you study hard and get a good education, and your homework has to be done. I also feel that there is time for you to be able to play baseball, but make sure the two don't interfere with each other. If baseball starts to interfere with your school work, you may have to re-evaluate how much time you're spending on baseball.

I can't remember having homework when I was eight years old. But if I did have homework then, I would have had to do it.

I play center field in Little League. In a game last year I tried to catch a fly ball, but I trapped it instead. The umpire thought I caught it and called the batter out. Should I have told him I really didn't catch the ball?—*Bryan Conners, 13*

The game of baseball is designed to rely on the umpire's judgment, and I know one of the problems in Little League is the number of umpires available.

From personal experience, there have been times in my career when a ball is thrown to me that I almost feel sure is a strike, and the umpire calls it a ball. And I don't tell him that I think it is a strike.

I have to rely on the umpire's judgment all the time, and the main thing is to make sure you're not trying to trick the umpire or being dishonest out there.

No. 51, Dale Murphy, blocks a shot for Wilson High School in 1974.

You tried to catch the ball, and he called it a catch. That was his judgment. There are going to be times when you actually catch the ball, and he thinks you didn't. So it's going to work both ways.

If I were in your position, and I didn't catch the ball and the umpire said that I did, and later in the game he asked me I would be honest. I would tell him that I didn't catch it. They usually just want to know, so they can make a better call next time.

You're to be commended for your honesty. You're not really dishonest for not telling the umpire what happened unless you want to volunteer it later.

One story I've heard involved an outfielder in a high school or college game. It was a big game, and the opposing team hit a home run, but it was hard to tell because of the fans and the sun. One of the umpires went out to check it out and asked one of the outfielders whether it was a home run. There was an opportunity to be honest or dishonest, and this fella said it was a home run.

It hurt his team, but it was the truth. And I am sure that has happened many times. But in the long run, you're not going to be hurt by being honest with the umpire.

————

Adult Coaches and Children

I received a letter the other day from a twelve-year-old child involved in athletics who complained about his coach yelling at him.

This is not the first such letter. So I thought I would take this opportunity to express some of my feelings about coaches of young athletes—particularly pre-high school athletes—and relate some of my own experiences.

I'm glad that my appetite for trying wasn't quenched after my first season in Little League when I struck out most of the time. I loved the game and I had fun playing it. I didn't really realize that I had had a bad season.

But coaches and parents, by their behavior, can make it a bad season for their kids.

It's a matter of perspective. The question is: What are we trying to accomplish? Are we trying to teach these kids winning at all costs, while sacrificing their development of self-confidence and self-esteem?

Here are some examples of the problem with youth athletics:

In a Little League game where the pitcher doesn't have very good control, the batter is told to go up to the plate and not swing, but look for a walk.

Well, that doesn't teach the kid how to hit the ball and doesn't give him the opportunity to find out if he *can* hit, and could hurt the kid's self-confidence.

A number of kids don't get to participate. I do admit to a lack of knowledge to the extent to which this is done here in the Atlanta metropolitan area. But there have been a number of instances in which kids go out for a sport, such as baseball or football, and sit on the bench the whole game. This certainly isn't fair.

I've received letters and attended a few Little League games in my years and have noticed situations where the coaches were yelling at the players: "Come on, Johnny! You swing like a girl!"

I've found that yelling usually scares the child. From personal experience, I know that if a coach yelled at me, I was more frightened than actually listening to his instruction.

Also, it belittles a person in front of a crowd and hurts his self-esteem. How many of us adults can handle being yelled at or reprimanded by our boss in the office in front of everyone?

A kid comes off a field after having a bad game and the parents berate him: "I don't even know why you play."

Families in the same neighborhood haven't spoken to each other for many years because of a dispute over a close call at the plate.

In youth football practice, a 7th grade player complained of a hurt arm during drills consisting of one-on-one, head-on contact. The coach made a few remarks concerning the amount of guts the kid had, got mad and told him to quit. The next day the kid came back with a cast on his arm.

With the youth football season just beginning and the baseball season ended, there are a few questions I want to ask all of us as parents and coaches:

Why do you want your child to participate in this sport?

What do you want to teach them as a coach?

Are we trying to teach them to have a good, positive attitude about themselves?

Do we, as coaches and parents, have the proper perspective as far as winning these Little League games is concerned?

The objective of youth sports should be for kids to go out and learn that sometimes you get a hit, sometimes you strike out; sometimes you win, sometimes you lose. But the most important thing is to go out and try.

Coaches and parents say we need discipline. I agree. It's valuable in life. But if our perception of discipline is yelling at them, disciplining their minds into a win, win, win attitude at the expense of self-confidence, where's the benefit?

As a professional baseball player for the Atlanta Braves, I am paid to get hits and win games. That is my job. I have a boss who pays for performance and expects it. We have to win to attract fans to the ballpark and to watch us on television because our boss has revenue obligations.

But Little League baseball, youth football, soccer or basketball should not be a job to a kid. Fun should come first.

The key to any game is enjoyment. Even in my profession, if I don't enjoy the game I'm going to quit. If kids can't go out and have fun, it's not right.

Let me ask you this: in ten years, which isn't too far away, are you going to be able to tell me the score of the championship game, or what your son's or daughter's average was?

Which is going to be more important in ten years: Whether that child hit .400 last baseball season or scored ten touchdowns last fall? Or whether he has confidence in his abilities because he learned in baseball, as in life, that he doesn't get a hit every time and sometimes strikes out?

Let's remember as coaches and parents that we are providing this opportunity for our kids to be involved in sports for them, not *us*. Let us not try to add a few extra stripes to our shoulders to win a few extra games when we could be jeopardizing some kid's development.

Some people stress that winning is everything, losing is shameful. You won't remember the score years from now, but a kid's hurt feelings can last a lifetime.

To convey to a child that it's the end of the world if he doesn't get a hit just isn't fair. It takes the fun out of playing the game. If a kid is burned out from youth sports—frustrated from giving up—who knows what he might give up on later in life.

I'm thankful that I've had some coaching, I think, that relayed to me the message of how to be successful. I can generally remember having a lot of fun playing baseball.

As I got into high school, I learned a little more as the demands grew. I was taught in high school that there were certain methods of success that we could apply to other areas of our lives. Not all of us were going to play major league baseball, and only one of us has from our high school team. But the guys on our team succeeded in other areas because they applied the lessons learned in high school baseball.

Many of us were given a chance to play and utilize our talents, and I had a lot of fun.

Winning and losing doesn't necessarily determine who is a success. Being successful is always trying. And enjoyment in life comes from having the confidence and self-esteem to try new things, not to be afraid to stumble or strike out, but to have the strength to get up and try again.

His eyes trained on the ball, Dale Murphy connects for a tenth-inning game-winning home run in 1985.—*Walker, Atlanta Journal & Constitution*

II. Hitting a Baseball

When you are up to bat, do you aim for the wall or do you have a special spot or do you just hit it?—*Stefani Schulman, 11*

I really don't try to hit a home run when I'm at bat. I just try to hit the ball and get a base hit.

If I think about hitting the ball to right field, that gives me the opportunity to hit the outside pitch. Then if the pitch is inside, I can hit the ball to left field.

But I try to think about hitting the ball to right field or over the second baseman's head. It doesn't always go there, obviously, but I think about hitting it there.

There are some players who can place the ball, but I haven't been able to do that. The main thing I try to remember is not to try to hit one over the fence every time.

Do you get the power in your swing from shoulders or your wrist?—*Doug Revis, 17*

That's a good question. It's a combination of a lot of things—not only your shoulders, but your legs, hips and arms. But in many ways, power comes from taking a proper swing—hitting the ball with the best part of the bat—and not necessarily swinging hard.

Usually, when I swing hard, I don't hit the ball as well. Sometimes I swing so hard my body—and my head and eyes—jerk slightly, and I can't keep my eyes on the ball. It's best to take a smooth, crisp swing. And I most often hit a home run when I'm not even thinking about it.

Of course, power in a swing can come just from strength. And a tall player often can get better leverage on the ball. At your age, you will notice that you can hit the ball farther and farther as you grow older and gain greater strength.

Do you grip the bat hard or soft? Do you hold the bat up high or down low to hit a home run?—*Joe Thomas, 13*

You certainly don't want to hold the bat too tightly. If you do, you won't be able to perform well because your muscles are too tight. A relaxed, loose grip is better, but you obviously want to be able to hold on to the bat.

The trademark is held up in this photograph of Dale taking a practice swing.—
Atlanta Braves

As for where to hold the bat to hit a home run, it doesn't matter whether the bat is held up high or down low. A lot of players who hit home runs hold their bats in many different positions.

Regardless of where you hold the bat, what you do need is a good, level swing to make contact. Most important, keep your eye on the ball and stay relaxed at the plate.

How did you feel when you hit your first home run in the major leagues?—*Laurie Clark, 16*

It was a big thrill, and it took me more than 100 times at bat to accomplish it. I hit my first home run off Randy Jones of San Diego in September 1977. I really couldn't quite believe I hit it that well—over the left-center field fence in Jack Murphy Stadium in San Diego.

I had hit twenty-six home runs in Triple A ball at Richmond before I came up to the Braves in Atlanta in September of that year. I remember that it was 1976, and I was really trying to hit a home run, and I only had a month to try. And I didn't do it.

So I was really happy to hit one the next year. Over those two Septembers I had played in about 30 games and had come to bat more than 100 times. Some guys—like Chuck Tanner, our manager—hit a home run the first time up.

How did you feel after your inside-the-park homer?
—Mitch Hollberg, 9

As soon as I hit the ball in that particular game in Montreal in 1984, I knew the ball was going near the fence. I made a mistake that you're never supposed to make as a baserunner: I didn't run hard to first base.

I thought to myself that he's going to catch it or it's going to be a home run. I didn't plan for the third possibility, hitting it off the wall. I ran to first kind of nonchalantly. I got halfway between first and second, and I thought, "If he misses it, I had better get at least a triple, or I'm going to be really embarrassed."

I hadn't run hard to first. That's where you've got to make up your ground to get your double or triple. You've got to run as hard as you can from home to first. I knew I hadn't hustled like I should.

I actually made it a closer play than it was. I had made a big mistake, and I was lucky the ball landed where it did. And it taught me a lesson.

Would you hit as well or better with an aluminum bat?—
Bradley James Robertson

There has been a lot of controversy about aluminum and wooden bats. A lot of players would say that the ball carries a lot farther with an aluminum bat than a wooden one when the ball is hit on the "sweet spot," the part where you're supposed to hit the ball. And I've also heard of studies that prove the ball doesn't go farther with an aluminum bat.

But personally, I do feel there is one instance where an aluminum bat would help me: when I don't hit the ball on the "sweet spot."

When a batter uses a wooden bat, and misses the "sweet spot," sometimes the bat will break and the ball automatically will not carry as far. When they first came out, aluminum bats would dent in the sweet part of the bat. Now they are as hard as a rock. An aluminum bat is now built so well that if you hit the ball on the handle or on the end of the bat, it won't break. So your chances of the ball carrying farther are greater if you hit the ball incorrectly.

So in that regard, I think the aluminum bat would help me. But I don't think you'll see us using aluminum bats in the major leagues.

Does it help to wear batting gloves?—*Edward Keith Navan, 6*

Personally, it helps me because it gives me a better grip. It just gives me the feeling here in Atlanta—especially with the humidity as high as it is—that I have a better grip on the bat.

It just feels comfortable to me. Some guys feel very uncomfortable with batting gloves, while others need two batting gloves. Sometimes I use two, but usually I just use one.

It's part habit and partly I feel that the leather, pine tar and resin mixed together give you a stickier grip. And if you've watched me play a little bit, you see that I throw my bat occasionally. It slips out of my hand, so I try to put as much pine tar and resin and Elmer's glue on my bat as possible.

(P.S.—I was just kidding about the Elmer's glue.)

Do you always hold your bat with the trademark on top so it won't break when you hit the ball?—*John Tarleton, 9*

I try to make sure I hold the label correctly and hit the ball with the right part of the bat. In baseball, you need every advantage you can get. And you need to take advantage of the wood and grain to hit the ball with the right part of the bat.

The label is a guide to how you should hold the bat. If you hit the ball where the wood in the bat is strongest, you should be able to hit the ball farther. Also, chances are that the bat won't break.

If I use a heavier and longer bat, will I get more power in my swing?—*Jerry Tassa, 8*

Not necessarily. I use a relatively short and light bat—34½ inches long and weighs 32 ounces. That's neither very long nor very heavy by major league standards.

If I were you, I would get a light bat that you felt you could swing faster. What we call bat speed is an important aspect of getting base hits or hitting the ball a long way. You need to be able to swing the bat through the strike zone fast enough to hit the ball hard.

If the bat is too heavy, you can't generate enough speed to get the bat through there. If a heavier bat would go just as fast as my 32-ounce bat, I would do it. But I just don't feel that I can, so I haven't gone to a heavier bat.

If I were your age, I would make sure I got a bat that was light enough, and then maybe get one lighter than that. You may even want to choke up on the bat because I choke up once in a while and I've seen Chris Chambliss and Bob Horner choke up. That will help you with both bat control and bat speed.

Who is the toughest pitcher you ever hit against?
—*Michael Matheny, 14*

Well, that's a tough question, because there are a lot of tough pitchers.

I've been on teams where we've had no-hitters thrown against us. One was by Ken Forsch of Houston and the other was by John Montefusco, when he pitched for the Giants. On those particular nights, those two were probably the toughest pitchers I've faced. Each pitcher has his own particular strengths, and on a given night, he can be tough to hit.

But the guy that comes to mind personally as being the toughest to hit was J.R. Richard of the Houston Astros. He's about 6-6 and threw between 95–100 miles an hour, had a real good slider and had pretty good control. But that was the problem: It was only "pretty good." You couldn't dig in against him.

He's probably the most overpowering pitcher that I have ever faced in my career. He was a true power pitcher who threw everything hard. And he was so tall you felt like he was about halfway to the plate when he put his foot down. What an imposing figure!

What pitch do you hit the best?—*Jason Diprima*

Probably the best pitch that I like to hit is just a little slower than a fastball and a little above the knees and right down the middle of the plate.

James Rodney Richard of the Houston Astros, whose pitches Dale found hardest of all to hit.—*Bud Skinner, Atlanta Journal & Constitution*

Unfortunately, I don't see that pitch very often. Usually, it's a fastball as hard as the pitcher can throw, or a curve or a slider. It isn't down the middle of the plate. The pitcher usually works it inside or outside.

The pitch I probably have the most trouble with is the slider, which is like a small curve ball. It comes up to the plate looking like a fastball, and just at the last minute curves away.

What is the best way to hit a curve ball when I'm up at bat?— *Dave Williams, 17*

You know, I wish I knew the answer to that one. As holder of the Braves' record for most strikeouts in a season, I certainly found out what a curve ball looks like.

I think the key to hitting a curve ball is keeping your weight back and your front shoulder in. Don't let that front shoulder fly open. Keep it tucked until the last moment.

Sometimes the pitcher is going to throw a good curve ball, and it may be tough to hit. Be ready on every pitch, however, because one of those times he might make a mistake. That's when you have to be ready! Above all, remember the all-inclusive theory of hitting that I use: Swing hard, in case you hit the ball. Keep working at it.

I've got a problem hitching when I bat. I used it in my ninth grade baseball season and won the batting title. The next season my coaches changed my batting style and I did awful. I couldn't hit and I felt down. I've never been hit with injuries, but I played hurt a little last year. It was more or less my worst year, and I think my injuries were on my mind. I need some good advice.—*Danny Tarrant, 16*

There's no question that injuries will affect you mentally as well as physically. In baseball, even a little injury to a finger can cause you problems with your concentration at the plate.

You need to be careful when playing with injuries, because you could get worse. I really wouldn't recommend playing with injuries at your age. It's just not worth it.

As for your batting style, remember your coaches are trying to be helpful. There's really nothing wrong with a hitch in your swing as long as you don't let that hitch, or dropping of your hands, interfere.

The higher up you play baseball, the harder the pitches will be. So you may have to make an adjustment for those pitches. It's best to let your hands move naturally when you stand up at the plate and not make any unnatural hitching movements. At a younger age, you are not at much of a disadvantage. But as you get older and face curve balls, you'll have to adjust.

One thing you, and the coaches, need to remember is that everyone

Pete Rose, whose limited physical skills did not keep him from becoming major league baseball's all-time leader in base hits.—*Bud Skinner, Atlanta Journal & Constitution*

does things a little bit differently. If everyone wanted to take the best hitter's example, everyone would hit like Pete Rose—and stand at the plate like Pete Rose. But it's not Pete Rose's stance, or the bat he uses, or any of that. Mostly, it's his mental concentration. That's where he differs from everyone else.

Each player stands in the batter's box differently. Take what the coaches teach you, practice it, and try to apply it to your own personal characteristics. But your coaches will teach you some basic things that have to be done.

Don't look at coaching as trying to change your way of doing things, but just trying to help you be more successful.

My dad is a coach. He makes me bunt a lot in practice. I just want to hit. What do you think?—*Jason Hicks, 6*

It's important to learn how to bunt.

That's one thing we, as professional ballplayers, don't practice too much. When you get into professional baseball, some people aren't called on to bunt as much as others. For instance, I'm not asked to bunt that much because of the position where I hit. But in high school, no matter where I hit in the lineup, whether I was the first hitter or anywhere on to the ninth hitter, it was important for me to know how to bunt.

Bunting is one of the key parts of the game, sacrificing yourself for the good of the team. It's a good weapon to sacrifice yourself to get a runner into scoring position or to surprise the other team and get a base hit. It's not easy to bunt, and you have to practice a lot. Rod Carew of the California Angels was one of the best bunters in the major leagues, and he practiced a lot to achieve that.

I do recommend practicing your hitting as well. Hitting is very important, too, and you will probably hit more times than you bunt. But nevertheless, you need to be proficient in bunting as well.

I am a natural left-handed batter. I am trying to practice switch hitting, but my arm will start hurting. Do you think I should stop or keep trying?—*Mike Durden, 14*

I think you should keep trying. Maybe it's just a matter of getting strength in your arm. If it's really hindering your throwing or being able to hit left-handed, you might want to slow down a little bit. But if it's just a matter of building up your strength and getting your muscles used to hitting the other way, I think you ought to continue to try to hit it for a while, because it's great to be able to switch hit, and the time to learn how is when you're young.

If you're a natural left-handed hitter, it's even better to be able to switch hit, because most of your hitting will be against right-handed

Lifting weights during the off-season.—*Atlanta Braves*

pitchers. If you can learn to hit right-handed, that's going to help keep you in the lineup and help, I think, get you more hits off those left-handers.

I wish that I were a switch hitter. Probably everyone in the league who's not a switch hitter wishes at one point in time that he had tried it when he was younger.

Last season I had two coaches telling me to stand in two positions at the plate. One told me to stand in front of the plate, and the other told me to stand behind the plate. I was confused. I originally stood on the side of the plate. Where at the plate am I supposed to stand?—*Brenda Johnson, 13*

I try to stand not too far back in the batter's box, but farther back than most hitters just because of my long stride and long legs—and big feet. I like to stand back and not too close to the pitcher because I get that much more time to see the pitch. I get a couple of more feet, which could be very important in seeing the pitch.

I stand a little bit back of the plate, but generally, I would recommend pretty much finding the best of both worlds—not too far back nor too forward. You need to stand in a place where you feel comfortable and where you are successful.

In baseball, some people stand so far away from the plate you would think they could never hit the ball. But they are comfortable, and they hit really well. George Brett, for one, of the Kansas City Royals, stands a long way away from the plate. And Bob Horner stands really close, and both are successful hitters.

No one can really determine what's the best place for you. Just find what's comfortable for you. Generally, it's the middle of the batter's box. And good luck this season.

Please tell me what kind of weight work I should do so I can get more "punch" in my hits. I am pretty much a spray hitter.—*Keith Favant*

It depends on your time and availability. If you have the time to work out, I think you need to make sure you do more things than just lift weights. The things that help you hit the ball best are stamina and, of course, strength. You need to be in good physical condition, which comes from jogging or playing racquetball or riding a bike.

Adult players need a good cardiovascular workout three times a week. And you need to lift weights three times a week as well. Your legs, upper body, stomach and back all need to be strong. Of course, you want to have strong wrists and forearms. But you get a lot of power from strong legs and a healthy back and stomach, too.

Also, you need some exercises for hitting. I swing a weighted bat and try to do some extra wrist exercises, whether it be wrist curls or something else. And a gripper is good to strengthen your hands and improve your power.

Do you think the crouch of your batting stance helps your batting average? Why?—*Tony Beckham, 17*

Sometimes I crouch, and sometimes I stand up a little straighter, but with all the different stances people use I don't think it is important to stand a certain way. Stan Musial, one of the best hitters of all time, used a crouch. Ted Williams, who some say was the finest hitter ever to play the game, stood straight up in the batter's box.

What is important, though, is to be comfortable, have good balance (which comes from slightly bending your knees) and be ready mentally to go up there and get a hit.

With experience you can experiment with different styles. But at your age, I would recommend keeping it simple: 1) be comfortable, 2) bend your knees slightly, and 3) go up there swinging!

I would like to know how to hit ground balls hard.
—*Jeremy Kendrick, 9*

Hitting a ground ball often depends on two things: 1) the angle of your swing, and 2) where you hit the ball with the bat. Sometimes you can swing up at a ball and hit a ground ball because you have hit the top of the ball with the bottom of the bat.

When I was younger, I wish I had hit more ground balls, because ground balls are better than fly balls unless you can hit them over the fence. Right now, as you are learning how to hit, it's best to hit line drives and ground balls. Then you have a better chance of getting a hit.

So what you want to do is take a good, level swing—some people might even say a slightly downward swing. Concentrate and think of trying to chop a tree down. That's the kind of swing you want to hit hard ground balls. That way you don't get underneath the ball. When you get underneath the ball, you are going to pop it up, and that's when you're in trouble.

I play shortstop, centerfield and pitcher, and I have a fear of being hit with the ball. When I'm at bat, what can you tell me so I won't fear that any more?—*Tracy Floyd, 11*

That fear is probably in every one of us who has played the game. A couple of things to remember: Usually, when a ball is being thrown at me, I am able to get out of the way. Also, it won't hurt for long if it does hit me.

That may not be comforting, but it is realistic to think that way, because if you play enough baseball you are going to get hit. That is definitely one of the challenges that you are going to have as you play baseball.

I wouldn't be helping you if I told you that you were never going to get hit, because everyone who has played baseball has been hit by the pitcher at some time.

The pitcher wants you to be afraid of the ball. He's going to have an advantage over you if he knows that you are.

I don't think you ever totally overcome the fear of being hit by a ball. A little fear, though, is good, because your body is aware of it. Sometimes you have to trust your mind and body to know that you will get out of the way. But too much fear is going to keep you from being able to perform.

If you concentrate on the ball, most of the time—not all of the time—you'll be able to get out of the way, because you'll see it coming.

And if you do see the ball coming toward you, duck your head and turn your shoulder so your back faces the pitcher. So if you are hit, it will be in the back. That's called the defensive roll.

I would like to know why you step out of the batter's box and hit the bat against your shoes every time you swing and miss.—*Matt Cassell, 8*

Sometimes when I swing and miss, I start to wonder if I can hit anything! So the first thing that comes to mind is that I need my confidence back. Well, I swing for my feet, and if I hit them, I know I can hit the ball!

I'm kidding you. There are actually two reasons: 1) To knock the dirt out of your spikes so you can get a firm stance in the batter's box, and 2) It's a habit. I've done it so much, sometimes I'll do it when there isn't any dirt in my spikes.

I think the secret to your hitting is to tap your hat. When I watched your games last season, you would tap your hat, and guess what? You hit a home run, of course. So please tell everyone on your team that if you tap your hat you usually get a home run.—*Amy Harris*

Every hitter has little habits, and some are superstitious and feel that for them to get a hit they need to do the same thing every time.

I don't have any superstitions, but I do have a routine that gets me ready. Golfers are often told that they need a routine before they approach their golf shots to get them mentally ready and set to go.

I just have a habit, and I appreciate your telling me that when I tap my helmet I hit the ball well. Now next season, please be sure to watch what I do when I strike out, and write me and let me know.

The long walk back to the dugout after a strikeout, 1982. But earlier in the game Dale hit a home run.—*George Clark, Atlanta Journal & Constitution*

When you get up to bat, do you ever get nervous?
—*Angela Scherer, 12*

I guess another way to ask that is: "Is there a time I've been to bat that I wasn't nervous?" I think every time I get to bat I get nervous.

Whether there are 5,000 or 50,000 people in the stands, or if it's a game-winning situation or a regular at-bat, I always seem to get those butterflies in my stomach.

How do you keep from getting mad or discouraged when you're having a batting slump?—*Danny Cavallo, 9*

Batting slumps aren't very much fun. I've been in a few slumps in my career, and everybody is bound to have them if you play baseball long enough.

I remember at one time things were going so bad Ted Turner asked me to get my eyes checked! Another time one of my teammates suggested I "take a surfboard up to the plate. At least you might make contact!" It was frustrating.

Some players, like Ted Williams (.344 lifetime batting average), probably never had a protracted "slump." But Ted Williams could hit a "BB" with a broom handle at midnight. And not too many guys can do that.

I've tried a lot of ways to get out of a slump: Different stances, different bats, a tighter or looser grip on the bat, hitting left-handed. (One time I was a switch-hitter, and my friends would say, "Murph is a switch-hitter. He hits three ways: Left, right and seldom.") I've tried a lot of things, but do you know what I've found to be the best way to get out of a slump? The key is what you're thinking about in the batter's box. Every time you get up there, no matter what happened last time up, you need to tell yourself, "I'm going to get a hit! Somehow, some way, because I've done it before, and I can do it again."

Sometimes it's not easy, I know, but that is the most important aspect of hitting—thinking positively when you're up there. This is when a coach or teammate can help your confidence as well, by encouraging you, saying, "I know you can get a hit. You can do it. I'm pulling for you!"

We need to help each other when things aren't so good and also help ourselves by thinking positively in all that we do.

Do you have to be corrected in batting practice ever?
—*Paul Johnson, 7*

I wish I could say that I never took a bad swing. But I have to be corrected every day in batting practice. I think it's good for someone to point out little things that will help your swing, as long as it's not done constantly.

Top, Dale steals second against the Houston Astros. Bill Doran leaps to take a high throw from the catcher. *Below*, Dale makes it back safely to first against Ray Knight and the Astros.—*Rich Addicks; Michael Pugh, Atlanta Journal & Constitution*

Sometimes the coaches will point something out; other times the players will talk to each other about what they notice in a batter's swing.

If baseball is your profession, you need a perfect swing every time. But it just doesn't always happen. You need to work and practice at swinging. And if you do it as many years as I have, you'll take a better swing with the bat. But there's always room for improvement.

I've been playing baseball for seven years. I practice all the time, but I still have a dip in my swing sometimes. Do you think practicing with a batting tee will help improve my swing?—*Larry Curl, 13*

Yes, I really do think batting tees are helpful. I think the tee-ball leagues are great because the batting tee is one of the best "teachers" we have.

With a tee, you can get your swing in a nice groove without having a pitcher or someone else. If a ball is sitting there on a tee, you should be able to hit every ball perfectly. Obviously, it's harder when someone is pitching. But with a tee you can practice. You can move the tee around to simulate an inside pitch or outside pitch or high or low.

Make sure you set the batting tee a little above knee height. As you hit the ball, make sure that you take a good, level swing and the ball comes off the tee a nice, low line drive. Also, you don't want to hit too much of the tee. Obviously, you want to hit the ball and maybe a little bit of the tee. But preferably, hit the ball only.

I think a tee is good. I use it during spring training and occasionally during the season. It really helps.

What does it take to become a good batting champion and base runner?—*Jeff Coogler, 14*

Being a good base runner surely comes in handy if you're to be a batting champion. Willie McGee of the St. Louis Cardinals won the batting championship in the National League in 1985 and he's one of the fastest runners in the league. If you're fast and a good base runner, you can sometimes still get a hit when you haven't hit the ball well.

A batting champion is someone who consistently hits well day in and day out (McGee hit over .350), and he can't have any serious injuries to keep him out for a very long time, because a batter must have 502 at-bats to qualify for the title.

Being a fast base runner is just a natural talent, but being a good base runner doesn't necessarily mean being fast. A smart base runner often knows what he is able to do—for example, not trying for third base because he knows he is not fast enough. So stopping at second can be good base running.

Willie Stargell, longtime home-run-hitting first baseman for the Pirates and more recently an Atlanta Braves coach.—*Bud Skinner, Atlanta Journal & Constitution*

I have seen fast runners who are not smart base runners. They will often take too much of a gamble because they think they can do this or do that. They don't think enough, and don't know how to use their speed to their advantage.

Most good base runners are not fast runners, but they know what they are capable of doing. They won't take a risk they shouldn't.

How do you steal? How do you know when to steal?
—Joey Wehmeyer, 9

I've never stolen as many bases as I did in 1983.

Until that year I never had a .300 batting average, so I had more chances on first base to think about stealing.

Also, I learned the important part about stealing is to get a quick jump off first base, and that is achieved by studying the pitchers.

I try to study the pitcher and get the first indication that he is going to throw to the plate. Then I try to start toward second base as soon as I can. Sometimes, you have to guess that he is going to throw toward home plate and try to steal the base.

I didn't even think about stealing thirty bases. I thought maybe I'd steal three bases, not thirty. But it worked out that way.

Whether I'll ever do that again, I don't know. It's a tough thing to predict because of my batting position in the lineup. If I were a leadoff hitter, I might have more opportunities.

When you are standing on a base (especially first) I have noticed you converse with the other team, and I was just wondering what is said by you and your competitors?
—Jamie Kennedy, 12

A number of things are said on the basepaths when there is a lull in the action. Sometimes, that's good; sometimes, that's bad.

One of our third base coaches didn't like us to talk too much to the other players because he likes to give us the signs: Whether to hit and run or steal or bunt. If you're over there talking to the first baseman, sometimes you're not looking at the third base coach.

So you've got to be a little careful, but it's usually small talk. You say, "Hi, how are you doing?" or "How are you hitting?" or something like that.

Willie Stargell was funny. He was always goofing around at first, cracking jokes and having a good time down there. Now he's our first base coach on the Braves.

Sometimes players try to get information about other players on the team. They will go down to the first baseman and say, "How's old so-and-so's arm?" or "Has he got a good curve ball?" They may be facing that pitcher the next night.

I always remember the time I got my first major league hit. It was against the Dodgers in Los Angeles. The hit was a little roller down the third base line, and I had to beat it out. I ran past first base and was coming back. The second thrill after getting my first hit was coming back to first and talking to a neat guy like Steve Garvey.

Steve said, "Congratulations, Dale. I hope you get many more."

But a lot of fielders will try to distract you and get your mind off what you're doing. They will be talking a mile a minute, and the next thing you know you miss a sign or get picked off first.

Also, fielders will confuse you as to how many outs there are. Sometimes the shortstop will say to the second baseman, "OK, there are two outs, right?" when there is only one out. So you have to be careful.

III. The Defensive Game

When a fly ball comes to the outfield, how do the players judge who should catch the ball?—*Matt Hilley, 8*

That's an interesting question, because as you have probably noticed, or experienced, there are balls that three people could catch. In the infield, literally everyone could catch a fly ball if he wanted.

We have what is called a priority system. We can tell by the ball's general direction who has what we call priority—whose ball it is if he can get to it. If he calls for it, then everyone else gets away.

Maybe you've noticed the shortstop going back for a ball, and all of a sudden he will run out of the way and let the outfielder catch it. That's because any ball hit in between the infielder and outfielder, the outfielder has first priority on catching it. The infielder has to get out of his way, because the outfielder has a better chance of catching it, since he is running forward and the infielder is running backward.

The priority system goes throughout the whole field. The shortstop and second baseman have priority over the third baseman and first baseman. First and third basemen have priority over the catcher, since the catcher is wearing a mask and all that gear. As for the pitcher, you seldom see him catch a popup.

You don't want to run into each other. On a fly ball to the outfield, you listen out closely to hear if anyone is saying, "I got it!" If you do hear that, that person has priority over you, and you let him take it.

If you watch the games closely, you'll notice players get out of the way. Sometimes, it doesn't work because one player can't hear the other, and that's why we collide, and sometimes get hurt.

How do you know what direction to go when a fly ball is hit?—*Dayla Robertson, 12*

That's a good question. It's something I practice, especially when I was switched to the outfield. Now I am getting a bit more used to it. I'm still practicing but not as much as I used to.

A mathematician analyzed what an outfielder has to go through to get right at that point to intercept the ball. He said it was amazing how fast your brain makes the calculations. But basically that's what it is: Practice, and your instinct. As soon as the ball is hit, somehow your mind starts telling you where you need to go to intersect the flight of the ball. Now sometimes you may be off a couple of feet, and you may not get to the ball or you may not be fast enough.

A bases-loaded sliding catch of a fly ball by Dale Murphy to close out an inning in 1983.—*Lanna Swindler, Atlanta Journal & Constitution*

When the pitch is made, and the ball is hit, I rely on two things:

1) The sound of the bat (the ball hitting the bat). There is a certain sound when the ball is really hit. There is another sound when you can tell the batter didn't hit the ball well. Either he hit it off the end of the bat or off the handle. When it sounds good, you know it's going to go a lot farther. If you take a little different angle or run a little bit harder, you account for that. If it doesn't sound good, you know you have to come in a few steps. Those are kind of tricky sometimes.

2) The flight of the ball. I know that if it is a low line drive, I have to come in for it. And if the ball takes a very high angle, it may come right to me. But if it is in between those two, it's probably going to be over my head, and I'd better start going back on it.

I play outfield and infield on my baseball team. Whenever the ball is hit real high, and I think I'm under it, it goes too far behind me or I reach back and fall. How could I stop this?— *Tommy Lezaj, 12*

When the ball's hit real high and you have a lot of time to get under it, it's best to go back a little bit farther than where you think the ball is going to land.

Judge the ball as best you can and go to the place where you think it's going to land. If you think it's going to land ten feet over your head and it's real high, go back thirteen or fifteen feet or so. Run as fast as you can. Then, as the ball starts coming down, you can move forward. That's if you have a lot of time.

Some people try to time it so they are on the run at the point where the ball is going to hit the ground. This is called drifting, where a player drifts over and catches the ball. That's the lazy way to catch a fly ball. Sometimes the ball is hit at an angle and there's no other way to catch it. But if you have time, get underneath it and wait for it.

When you are going for a fly ball over your head, it's important to turn your body to the side and run for the ball. Never run backwards with your back to the fence.

The next time you go to a game, watch how our outfielders run after a ball that's hit over their head. You can run back toward the fence with your eyes still on the ball. Don't backpedal. It's too hard to keep your balance while running backwards.

Dale leaps high but can't hold onto a drive by the Chicago Cubs' Leon Durham in 1983. The scorer ruled it a triple. Note the sunglasses Dale is wearing. *Below*, Dale held on to this one, making a diving catch and then scrambling to his feet to throw out a baserunner at second.—*Ray West; Rich Addicks,* Atlanta Journal & Constitution

When we have a game, it will start at 5 p.m. and the sun is still up. I have a pair of sunglasses, but when a fly ball comes I don't have time to take them off my forehead onto my eyes.—*Eugene Herrington, 13*

We have sunglasses that are hinged so you can flip them up or down. They are not regular sunglasses on your forehead that are pulled down over your eyes when you need them.

I have no idea where they are found. What I would suggest is that you call sporting goods stores and find out where you can find some baseball flip-down sunglasses.

They do help a lot, but you've got to learn how to use them. When we have a game and the sun is out and I flip down the glasses, it takes some getting used to. All of a sudden everything is dark—very dark— and the baseball is a little dark spot.

The glasses won't help on those balls directly in the sun. You can see the ball that is off to the side of the sun easily, but it takes practice.

When the outfield is wet, how do you play a ball hit to you differently than if you were in a dry outfield?
—*Leigh Anne Bumgardner, 15*

Some summers we have a lot of rain at the stadium, and players have to be really careful.

If the field is wet, a player has to take a little more time and be a little more careful in catching a ball in the outfield. Lots of times the ball will skip on wet grass instead of taking a normal bounce. Also, the ball is wet and you have to be careful throwing it.

Sometimes it's going to land in a puddle. Then you have to be sure when you lean down to grab the ball that you're going to get it.

Of course, if it's a situation where you have to throw the runner out at home plate, you can't afford to take your time. You just do the best you can. If you play it too carefully, you're not going to have a chance to do anything.

But if it's a situation where you just have to catch the ball, you take your time and concentrate extra hard on what kind of hop it's going to take, and make the best throw you can, because it will be soaking wet.

Baseball is hard to play in the rain. That's why if it's coming down too heavy we don't play.

What is the most difficult position besides the pitcher to play in baseball?—*Sean Mitchell, 8*

It's hard for me to tell. I was a catcher at one time, and that's definitely one of the most demanding positions. The catcher takes a

Dale as a young catcher for the Braves against Dave Winfield and the San Diego Padres. *Below,* Dale slides for the plate as the Cubs' catcher Jody Davis moves to tag him out, while Rafael Ramirez, who has signaled to Dale to hit the dirt, looks on.
—*Photo below by Michael Pugh, Atlanta Journal & Constitution*

beating behind the plate. Sometimes he gets run over by a runner, or a foul ball hits him in the mask, or foul tips hit his fingers. All kinds of things happen.

So catching—day in and day out, I would say—is probably the toughest position, next to being a pitcher. They require totally different skills, so it's hard to compare them. A pitcher pitches every fourth day; a catcher tries to catch every day.

Pitching, overall, I think is the toughest. But next in line would have to be catching, because of how tiring it gets and how much of a strain it is on your legs to bend up and down on every pitch.

Why did you switch from first base to outfield?
—Vincent Russell, 13

I hurt too many shortstops trying to make a double play by hitting them in the shins with my throws.

To tell you the truth, so many ground balls missed my mitt and hit me in the chest that they thought it might be good to put me in the outfield where the balls roll a bit slower.

Those are the two main reasons.

My defense just wasn't good enough at first base or catching really to have me there in the lineup. So Bobby Cox, the manager then, and Ted Turner gave me a chance in the outfield.

It was actually by popular demand of our whole infield to "get Murphy out of there."

If you miss a ball, and somebody yells at you, what should you do?—*Adam Blomberg, 8*

That's happened to me quite a bit. As long as you play baseball, as long as you're involved in any sport, you're going to make mistakes. The only way you can make a mistake is to be involved and be out there playing.

That's the way I look at it. If I weren't out there playing, I wouldn't make any mistakes. But I wouldn't accomplish anything, either.

I really don't do anything when someone yells at me or I hear boos from the fans. I just try to not let it affect me, because ruining my concentration is the worst thing that can happen. Just realize you can't go out there and do everything perfectly every time on the field.

Unfortunately, some people sometimes don't realize that if they were out there, that same thing might happen to them. Sometimes people yell at you for making a mistake. And sometimes it's your coach, sometimes it's a fan, and sometimes it's another teammate. That's unfortunate, because these people need to know that the best

Playing first base, Dale stretches to take a throw.—*Atlanta Journal & Constitution*

way to help a guy overcome his mistakes is by encouraging him. And, usually, we know when we have made an error.

What's needed are more people, especially teammates, to encourage someone who's made a mistake, by bolstering his confidence by saying something like, "Don't worry. We'll get them next time." That helps more than yelling at him, because he already feels bad enough. When you get that kind of encouragement, you really want to do better the next time.

And if you don't get that kind of encouragement, you need to encourage yourself. Tell yourself, "I've made a mistake, but I'm not going to do that again."

I play baseball, and my last game the coach said throw it to the pitcher, and the crowd said throw it to third, and I'm confused. What should I do?—*Blake Higgins, 8*

In your particular question, it's hard to tell who you should have followed because in Little League, sometimes even in the major leagues, we get conflicting opinions as to which might have been the proper play.

I've found that what helps me the most when I'm in the outfield—and this applies to any position—is to think to myself, "If the ball is hit to me, what am I going to do with it?" Then you are prepared. If you are a catcher, you think, "If a runner starts to steal, what am I going to do with the ball?"

What you need to do is prepare yourself before each pitch so you're ready for that situation. Then you won't have to think about it because you've already decided what you're going to do.

If you're an outfielder and there is a runner on second, you think, "If there is a ball hit toward me, I'm going to throw it home and try to get the runner out."

In a major league game, an announcer might say, "That was a quick decision!" on a certain play. Well, we've already been through a lot of such plays. And I'll guarantee you that almost every time that player had already thought of that particular play before he did it. If he had tried to decide during the play, it would have been too late.

When you played first base, did you catch the ball with one hand or both hands?—*Jeff Henard, 14*

You've probably had a lot of experience catching. At 14, you've probably learned how to catch the ball with two hands. I always recommend to kids that they learn how to catch the ball correctly with two hands.

At first base, you'll see a lot of professional ballplayers catch the ball with one hand. They have played so much baseball that they are able to catch it with one hand. But you will notice a lot of infielders catch a ground ball with two hands, especially if it's a little tough.

In the outfield and at first base, you are able to stretch out your body longer if you reach with one hand. You actually don't want to catch every ball with two hands. If you're playing first base, for example, and a fielder throws the ball way to your right, you are able to stretch farther with one hand than trying to catch it with two.

Does it hurt your hands when you catch the ball?
—*Ryan Thomas, 8*

Yes, it does—sometimes even when the ball is not hit hard. But now I've learned to catch the ball in the webbing of my glove.

An outfielder has a much larger glove than an infielder. Outfielders don't have to get rid of the ball as quickly as an infielder does. We don't have to turn the double play and fire it to first base. That's why an infielder's glove is much smaller.

The outfielder needs a larger glove because he's often running at full speed and diving and hitting the ground. He needs the ball to stick in the webbing of his glove.

Usually, it doesn't hurt when I catch the ball, because I usually get it in the webbing between the forefinger and thumb. Every once in a while I will catch a ball in the palm of the glove and that can hurt. But the pain doesn't last too long.

I got a new glove for Christmas. How should I break it in?—
Holly Sawchuck, 8

A lot of players break in their gloves different ways. A couple of ways that come to mind that I don't necessarily support:

Some guys will take a couple of balls and put them in the pocket of the glove and wrap it up with string to the shape they want to make it. Then they dip it in water and get it completely soaking wet. They they stick it out in the sun for a couple of days to dry. The thought is that the pocket will be formed. Your glove will be as hard as a rock, but eventually that leather will loosen up.

Other guys put shaving cream all over their mitts because of the softening lanolin and other things in shaving cream that will loosen the mitts up. But the main problem is getting that leather loose.

You want your glove to last as long as it can. In professional baseball we don't need our mitts to last as long, because we are supplied equipment.

All I put on my glove is a little bit of mink oil in the center and around some of the webbing, where it will loosen it up a bit.

That's what I suggest for you: A little mink oil, soften the leather up and then just play a lot of catch. And keep patting your fist in there to get the pocket right where you want it.

I've noticed when you are in the outfield that you inspect the grass every now and then—pulling and examining the weeds. Have you had training in the area of weeds?—*Blakely Dinwitty*

I've played baseball since I was eight years old so I've had a lot of experience standing out in the grass and weeds. It's amazing that you asked that question because I did a report on weeds when I was in the eighth grade.

Now whenever I get a chance to go to different ballparks, I just kind of look down, out of habit, and check the weeds. It's amazing the kinds that grow in California, the kinds that can't grow in the South.

A few weeks ago, as a matter of fact, I actually pulled one of the weeds out of our outfield in Atlanta.

That's one of the reasons I hate AstroTurf. It's just so boring. I see the same thing night after night. I think they ought to come up with some Astro Weeds so I can at least start to classify them and put them in their proper place in the weed kingdom.

Actually, pulling weeds is just a nervous habit. Sometimes when I examine the grass in Atlanta, it's because there's a piece of AstroTurf covering the sprinkler in centerfield. I kind of check it a lot to make sure it's down so I won't trip over it.

What was your most memorable play or game?
—*Michael Ferrara, 11*

One of the most memorable plays was in 1983 when we were playing the Dodgers in Dodger Stadium, with Len Barker pitching.

In the middle of the game, with us leading, Pedro Guerrero hit a pitch to right-center field and I jumped up against the fence and caught the ball, and we went on to win the ballgame. It was almost a home run and we were still in the pennant race at that time.

One of the most memorable games for me came against the San Francisco Giants one Sunday afternoon in 1979 when I hit three home runs. I'll never forget that because it was such a thrill. And, of course, there was the 18-inning game against the Giants in which I went 0-for-8 with four strikeouts. That was the worst game of my life. I'll never forget that one, either.

Dale and Pedro Guerrero at Dodger Stadium in Los Angeles.

IV. It's How You Play the Game: The Right Attitude

Please tell me which pitcher and team you like to play against the most.—*Nathan Espy, 7*

I would have to say it's always exciting to play a team like the Los Angeles Dodgers because of their tradition, and they always have a good team. It's kind of like playing the New York Yankees in the American League—an established team with good players. There's a lot of excitement and a lot more attention focused on the game when you play them.

I like playing in Dodger Stadium as well because it's one of the most beautiful stadiums to play baseball in. It's one of the few stadiums built just for baseball. So it's fun to go to Los Angeles and play the Dodgers there.

As far as pitchers are concerned, it's really hard to pick out one that I would like to hit against, because some nights I might go out and get three hits off the guy, and the next time I face him he might strike me out three times.

I can think of a lot of pitchers that I don't like to hit against. Every night there's a pitcher who's tough, so as a hitter I have to remember not to like the pitcher . . . So I don't like any of them.

Do you think the National League should switch to designated batters for their pitchers?—*Jeannie Coltrane, 13*

No, I don't. I'm basically a traditionalist as far as baseball is concerned. I like grass fields and the older ballparks, and I like the traditional-looking uniforms. I enjoy baseball and its history. I think one of the great things about the game is that it hasn't changed much over the years.

I feel that the designated hitter takes away a lot of the tradition of the way the game is played. I guess my father-in-law puts it best when he says baseball is a game the fan can get involved in, and it's slow enough where the fan can make his own decisions. If the manager uses a pinch hitter and it works out and you agreed with him, you can take pride in agreeing with him. And if it doesn't work out, and you disagreed with him, you can second-guess the manager.

But one of the big decisions a manager faces is when to take out a starting pitcher when he is pitching well. Do you let him hit or do you pinch hit? With a designated hitter and the pitcher not batting, that decision is taken away from the manager. He never has to pinch hit for his starting pitcher, and I think that's a big part of baseball.

What is your favorite park to play in besides Atlanta?
—Keven Shockley, 12

I enjoy the older ones, like Chicago's Wrigley Field, because of the tradition there, and also Los Angeles' Dodger Stadium. It's one of the few ballparks built for baseball only, and it's a beautiful place to play.

I also enjoy playing in Philadelphia's Veterans Stadium because the fans are close to the field.

Would you rather play in a dome or in a regular stadium?—
Maury Kimball, 11

I'd rather play in a regular stadium. I enjoy playing outside rather than in the Astrodome (or the Kingdome or Metrodome in the American League). I also enjoy playing on natural grass more than I do AstroTurf. I think it's a more traditional game on the grass. It's also a lot easier on the knees and legs.

Sometimes, too, it can be hard to see a fly ball in a domed stadium. When the background is the roof of the dome, it sometimes blends in with the color of the ball and it's hard to pick up. Also, in the Astrodome, for instance, the air doesn't carry the ball as well as some of the outside parks. I always enjoy playing where it's easier to hit a home run.

I would like to know what you do in your spare time, like when you travel to Los Angeles to play the Dodgers.
—Henry Collins, 11

Los Angeles is a unique example. Since Nancy and I have been married, my in-laws have come to Los Angeles from Utah the last few years to see the games. So my time has been spent with them.

Basically, there isn't much to do in most of the downtown areas where we stay. You really don't want to go out sightseeing too much (like in Los Angeles to go to Disneyland too many times) because you get worn out. You want to reserve your strength for the game.

So you don't have a chance to go out and see too many of the sights. Since we often have a late night game, I think most of the guys usually sleep in a little bit, get up and eat, and maybe walk around the shops in the area. You try to get your bones and muscles loosened up and the blood flowing.

There have been times when I have had an off-day in a city like San Diego where I rented a sailboat and went sailing. That was enjoyable. And in New York I have seen the Statue of Liberty and other tourist sites.

But most of the days on the road consist of walking around downtown, and all the downtowns seem to be the same.

Do ballplayers have a curfew?—*Tanya Moss, 17*

Yes, in spring training and during the season we're given certain rules about when to be in bed. And they are pretty much the same for most teams in the majors. Most of the managers I have played for expect a player to take care of himself.

Not being able to perform is the result of not really taking good care of yourself. There aren't any really rigid and strict rules, only guidelines for us. But most of the guys can take care of themselves and realize that if they are not in shape they are not going to be able to perform. And that is going to be the punishment.

What do you do on off days?—*Rich Diprima, 13*

Well, that depends. If I'm home, I try to make sure I am around the house. Nancy and I usually have something planned. We usually try to do something together as a family—not necessarily camping or fishing. It's nothing elaborate.

And I like to take Nancy out on off days. It's one of the few evenings during the season that we get to spend with each other.

When I'm on the road, sometimes I'll play golf, take in a movie or sometimes I'll just relax and try to recuperate.

One time in San Diego I went sailing. Other guys went to the beach or to the zoo or Sea World. But on our last off day in San Diego—a Saturday—it rained. So I did some shopping and just relaxed.

I just want to ask you if you ever get tired of baseball.
—*Toby Adcock, 10*

I do get physically tired from traveling or playing 162 games, and I'll be the first to admit that I don't mind taking some time off after the season.

Pete Rose has been known to say that after the seventh game of the World Series he wished opening day were tomorrow. But I don't mind taking a little break from baseball, although a couple of weeks after the season is over I'm kind of eager to get started again.

As soon as I get tired of the game, I'll probably retire. But I still feel like a kid out there, and I'm doing basically the same thing I have been doing since I was eight years old.

Some day, I know, I'll have to get a job. I just enjoy playing. But I do enjoy the off-season and the time not thinking about baseball, too.

A dejected Dale Murphy walks off the field as the Braves lose to the New York Mets at Atlanta–Fulton County Stadium in 1981.—*Bud Skinner, Atlanta Journal & Constitution*

What do you like least about your job as outfielder of the Braves?—*David Cork, 15*

One of the things I least like about it is that I have to run so far to the dugout. Sometimes I wish I were at first or third base. Then I would just walk twenty feet to the dugout. I'm getting old and can't run that far.

But the toughest thing in the outfield is the wind or the sun or both. That's what I don't like about playing the outfield.

As far as my occupation is concerned, two things come to mind:

1) Traveling. I wish we could play all home games. Staying close to home would be enjoyable. If I could complain, I guess that's what I would complain about . . . and I like to complain.

2) Playing on Sunday. I firmly believe in Sunday being a day of rest. We should rest from our labors, attend church and be with our family that day. Sunday should be a day to strengthen ourselves spiritually and physically for the coming week.

I understand we all have our decisions as far as our occupations are concerned, and some do require work on Sunday. And unfortunately, I do do that. But that's not something I enjoy.

Could you tell me about the training you go through in winter?—*Rodney Anderson, 15*

I've found how important the winter is to a ballplayer. If you're in good shape physically, it's going to help you mentally.

Being in good condition is going to help you when you get injured, because you'll be able to recover faster.

I usually try to take some time off in the fall to relax and let everything heal from the season.

I like to lift weights, and I have an exercise bicycle at home, because I've had two operations on my left knee, and if I do a lot of running it does aggravate it. And I keep in shape chasing Chad, Travis, Shawn and Tyson all winter.

As for baseball hitting and throwing, I take my time working into it slowly, because we have six weeks of spring training.

But being prepared is half the battle—feeling that you're ready to go.

When you start spring training, how long does it take you to get back in the groove after being off for so long?
—*Donnie Hemphill, 14*

For me it takes quite a while—at least a week of batting practice and another week to ten days of games. Some guys have a natural type of swing, and it doesn't take them long to get their timing down.

The compact swing of Bob Horner, ready to hit for distance from the first day of spring training onward. *Below*, the Braves take calisthenics to limber up. Chris Chambliss, No. 10, is behind Dale, and Pete Falcone behind him.—*Joey Ivansco, Atlanta Journal & Constitution*

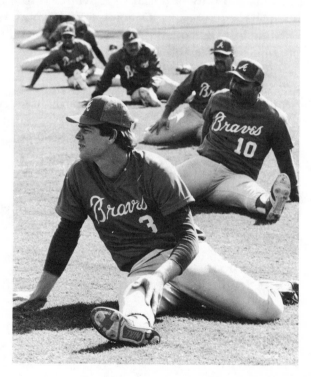

Bob Horner is a perfect example. He comes down to spring training and looks good swinging when he first steps into the batting cage.

For me, it takes a while before I feel comfortable hitting a baseball again. I guess I could hit a little more in the winter, but I just like to stay in good physical condition. Hitting is all timing and reflexes.

As for fielding, I've never really gotten in the groove. But for hitting and fielding, I think it's important now that players go down to spring training *in* shape. I think the attitude used to be that players went to spring training to *get into* shape.

If a player is in shape, he can take his swing and field balls and work on his skills. But if he isn't in shape, he will get tired after a few swings and can't work on improving himself.

What should you do to get warmed up?—*Chad Beacham, 9*

I think that is one of the most important parts of the game. Running a few sprints before the game helps us to get our blood going and our legs loose.

What we try to do about half an hour before the game is stretch out our legs, our lower backs, shoulders and arms. We do that in the clubhouse before we come out onto the field. Paul Mastropasqua is our strength and fitness coach who leads us through some exercises before we go out. When we get out on the field, we jog a few easy sprints to get our legs loose. Then we play catch to get our arms loose.

Twice I've learned the consequences of not warming up properly. During two years in spring training I pulled the quadriceps muscle in my leg. It wasn't even a bad pull and it still hurt. I pulled a back muscle just recently in Los Angeles during batting practice because I think I didn't warm up properly. I'm one of those guys who thought he could never pull a muscle because he never had.

But it's important that before you undertake any athletic endeavor—jogging or tennis or anything—you give those muscles a warmup. It only takes ten to fifteen minutes.

On a game day, how early do you get to the ballpark, and what do you do to prepare for the game?—*David Taylor, 6*

I leave for the ballpark around 3:45 and try to get there about 4:45. Batting practice usually starts between 5:15 and 5:30 and lasts about an hour. We just go out there and take a few swings and try to get loose.

Then we go back into the clubhouse while the visiting team takes practice. Sometimes we'll come out and take infield practice, which is a chance for us to get our arms loose and catch a few fly balls.

After that we go into the clubhouse and usually have about 45 minutes and relax a little bit before the game. We try to get our

"Get mean!" Manager Chuck Tanner of the Braves tells Rafael Ramirez in pre-game practice. *Below*, nine stitches were taken in Dale Murphy's left hand after he gashed it on the fence against the Mets in 1986. The next evening he pinch-hit a home run.—*Joey Ivansco; Calvin Cruce, Atlanta Journal & Constitution*

thoughts together on who might be pitching or how to play some of the other players defensively and discuss any last-minute adjustments before the game.

The first time we play a team during the season we have a meeting to go over the players. There is also a special meeting between the pitchers and catchers on how they want to pitch to certain players.

Then we have a little stretching program where we stretch our muscles in the clubhouse. Then we come out ten to fifteen minutes before the game time to jog a few sprints to try to loosen our muscles up and get the blood going a little bit.

What do you do to relax before a game?—*Amy Seabolt, 12*

We have quite a bit of time at home before the game, but there are a number of things we do to relax at the stadium.

I usually find something to eat . . . but seriously:

We have a TV room where we can watch a show before the game. Or a player can sit down and read the paper, read a book, enjoy a snack or just sit and chat with the other players about the pitcher for that night's game.

It's good to always keep your mind occupied. But since we play so many games—162—you can't drain yourself emotionally for each game. You try to find a steady emotional level that you're able to keep day in and day out. And you try to conserve your energy before the game. About 20–30 minutes before game time, we start our stretching exercises to get ready.

When games go into extra innings and don't get over until late in the night, do the ballplayers have trouble staying awake?—*Tanya Moss, 16*

Well, we've certainly had our games that lasted way into the night. We have had some with rain delays and some with extra innings. But we really don't have any trouble staying awake while we are playing.

One night we stayed out there until past 3:30 in the morning when we played the New York Mets. In a case like that, we are a little tired, but we don't have any trouble keeping our eyes open. We're still moving around and the adrenaline is still flowing to keep us going.

Actually, I had trouble going to sleep after that game with the Mets. The game went 19 innings. I was tired, but it was hard to relax, especially after a long, close, nip-and-tuck game. I was pretty tired the next day after having not slept well after that long game.

It definitely messes up my schedule a little. But during the game itself, I was into the game and didn't notice so much that I was tired—until I looked up at the clock and noticed it was 3 a.m. Then I thought, "Hey, this thing's getting a little late."

Is it difficult with all your success to keep a sense of humility?—
Tracey Holley, 14

I've really been grateful for the limited amount of success that I've achieved. I've done some things right, and I've done some things wrong. But I've found that baseball is a humbling game in many respects. Even if you hit .300, that means you're only getting three hits out of every ten times at bat, and seven of those ten times you did something "wrong."

I think there is a lot of built-in failure in the game anyway. When you don't do what you're supposed to do, it keeps you humble. There's always someone who can strike you out or someone who can make a good play on you defensively. As far as the game is concerned, I don't have any trouble reminding myself that I'm a human being out there and I'm going to make mistakes.

An idea that I always try to keep in mind is that I'm no different from anybody else on this earth, except that on my job, I happen to wear No. 3 for the Atlanta Braves. I realize this doesn't put me above anyone else because I have a different job. I try to remember that and it keeps things in perspective for me.

As a baseball player, as an entertainer, sometimes your perspective can change because people want your autograph or want you to endorse their products. So you have to be careful not to change your perspective and think, "I must be a pretty unique individual."

The only thing unique about us is our job. So I have no reason not to have a sense of humility as far as being a baseball player is concerned.

About how many interviews do you do a week? And do they ever annoy you?—*Susan Vess, 14*

It comes and goes. It really depends on how I'm doing. If I'm doing well, I usually get a lot of interviews. And if things aren't going so well, I get a lot of interviews, too. Usually most players have at least one interview after the game to talk about what happened. The sportswriters in Atlanta who cover baseball are there every day. Occasionally, there will be people from out of town or from a magazine.

During the season, it differs from week to week for me. There have been some weeks when I had an interview every day before the game. As far as it bothering me, it never really bothers me to give an interview. The only problem I have is that I need to be careful with my time at the stadium. So sometimes I have to tell the reporter that I have to go to batting practice now or that I don't have the time.

It's not that I mind doing the interview. I recognize that reporters have their jobs to do. I want to accommodate them as far as possible, as long as it doesn't interrupt my time schedule—my job—at the ballpark.

The hard part is talking to reporters after we have lost a game or I didn't play very well. That's not very much fun. But I try to answer the questions.

What is the strangest thing anyone has ever asked you to autograph?—*Brandi Branson, 15*

I was playing in Richmond, Virginia, a few years ago. I hit a foul ball, and this guy in the stands tried to catch it. But it hit him right in the chest, and he wanted me to autograph the bruise. And that's the truth. By the way, I think I autographed it.

A few months ago, there was an article in the Atlanta paper about the way you feel about women in the locker rooms. Well, what I want is to hear it straight from you. How do you feel? Why do you feel this way? Also, is there anyone else on the team who feels the same way?—*Lisa Taylor, 13*

First of all, I thank the baseball commissioner, who a few years ago took a stand on the issue of women in the locker room. There were some women reporters who wanted access to the New York Yankees' locker room because they wanted to do a story about the game. The Yankees wouldn't let these women reporters in the locker room, so they challenged that decision in court.

I'm thankful that the commissioner at that time, Bowie Kuhn, felt that the Yankees were right. The commissioner, on behalf of baseball, took the stand that it wasn't right to have women in men's locker rooms and that it was an infringement on our rights as players to privacy. The case went to court in New York, and unfortunately the judge ruled that any reporter, whether male or female, gets equal access to the players.

Personally, I—as well as many other players—feel the judge made the wrong decision. In giving what he felt was equal rights to one group of people, he took away my right to privacy. There are many Braves and others who support this position. You see, the locker room is where we change our clothes and shower after a game. Basically, it's no place for a woman to be. I just feel that it's a moral question.

I've had some women reporters come up to me and say, "What'll we do if we want to cover baseball and there's this obstacle? How do we overcome it?"

I would probably tell them what I would tell my little daughter if she wanted to do that: "Until something is worked out, find another job, because a men's locker room is no place for a woman to be."

Possibly there are some solutions to the problem. One of the things that is tossed around, which is used in the NFL, is a separate interview room where all the reporters go to talk to the players. There might be other solutions that I am not aware of.

Bruce Benedict and Dale signing autographs.

I don't object at all to being interviewed by a woman reporter. Even though they are allowed in the clubhouses, I won't talk to them while they are in there. But I will talk to them outside the clubhouse, because I don't want to inhibit a woman reporter from doing her job.

Do you think there will ever be women to play major-league baseball, and would you mind if women play?
—*Marie Dodd, 12*

A lot of fans have written in, asking that question.

I would be the first to encourage anyone, man or woman, to pursue those worthwhile goals that they want to achieve. I can't really say that there will never be any women playing major-league baseball. Looking at past history, however, I don't feel that it would be any time soon. A couple of thoughts come to mind:

1) In over 100 years of baseball there haven't been any women in the major leagues.

2) Each year between 500 and 600 players are drafted. These are guys the scouts believe have some potential to make it in the major leagues, but only about three to four percent of them get to see any major-league action.

3) Most of the major-league ballplayers have been playing since they were eight or nine years old and have a lot of training.

I'm not saying it can't be done. I'm just saying it hasn't, and those are possibly some of the reasons.

There are a lot more girls playing Little League baseball now than when I played, and that is great. It takes a lot of work to make it.

Now there are some professional women fast-pitch softball players who wouldn't have any trouble striking me out, but that is a different sport.

I would welcome anyone, man or woman, who could contribute to the cause, and I think anyone on the Braves would feel the same way. If there is a woman out there who can make it in the majors, I am sure the scouts will sign her.

Does it affect your play when one of your friends is traded?— *Vincent Russell, 14*

No, I don't really think it affects my play so much. I think most of us are so used to baseball players being traded. Sure, we become friends and it's tough seeing someone leave. But being traded can be a good thing. It means at least he gets a chance to play, and maybe a better chance with another team. Take my friend Larry McWilliams, for example. We played together in the minor leagues. When the Braves traded him to the Pittsburgh Pirates he became a star.

Dale receives the congratulations of manager Chuck Tanner after hitting a home run.—*Calvin Cruce, Atlanta Journal & Constitution*

Sometimes I'm happy for some of my teammates who've been traded, because it may be a better situation for them, and of course we're getting another guy who may help us. Think how much Ken Griffey's bat added to our team when we got him from the Yankees last summer.

Then there are some who may be released, which means they are through playing baseball. Another organization may pick them up, but it's tough to see your friends not get a chance to play.

But that's part of the game, and we've all seen it and experienced it. We realize that we are paid to go out on the field and play hard and must put those things behind us.

Does a new manager affect the way you play?
—Vincent Russell, 14

A new manager may have a different style and different philosophy as far as managing the team, but individually it doesn't affect the way you play.

For example, one manager may emphasize stealing bases while another might want you to hit more home runs. But as far as how an individual plays, the manager may want to change your style of hitting or try to work on your hitting or pitching to help your technique a little bit.

But most players generally play the same under all managers as far as hustling and working hard and attitude toward the game. That doesn't change.

Why is the spit ball illegal?—*Kim Houston, 17*

Here's what the rule book says:
"The pitcher shall not:
"(1) Bring his pitching hand in contact with his mouth or lips while in the 18 foot circle surrounding the pitching rubber . . .
"(2) Apply a foreign substance of any kind to the ball.
"(3) Expectorate on the ball, either hand or his glove.
"(4) Rub the ball on his glove, person or clothing.
"(5) Deface the ball in any manner.
"(6) Deliver what is called the 'shine' ball, 'spit' ball, 'mud' ball or 'emery' ball. The pitcher, of course, is allowed to rub the ball between his bare hands . . ."
The penalty: The pitch is called a ball, and the pitcher is warned. A second offense in the same game, and the pitcher is ejected.

There are many things a player can do to give him the advantage illegally—whether it's with a baseball or with a bat. Some guys have been accused of putting cork inside the end of the bat, which makes the ball travel farther when it's hit. Using a spit ball or putting Vaseline

Glenn Hubbard, the Braves' feisty little second baseman in action.—*Kenneth Walker, Atlanta Journal & Constitution*

on the ball gives the pitcher an unfair advantage, too. Also, scuffing the ball or doctoring it will make it move differently. There are certain pitchers accused of throwing illegal pitches who get watched a little bit more closely than others.

There are many times when we as players silently accuse another pitcher of possibly doing something to the ball. The spit ball moves differently from any other pitch, and you can really tell. You go back to the dugout after missing a pitch and say, "Man, that ball did something pretty funny."

All the ball needs to do is move a couple of inches when it's coming in at 85 miles an hour, and you're going to miss it. That's all the pitcher wants you to do.

I would appreciate knowing the proper umpire's decision in the following play:

I was catching behind home plate with a runner on third when the pitcher threw a wild pitch. I threw my mask off and turned quickly to recover the wild pitch.

As I turned around for the ball, I knocked the umpire over, who went head over heels and fell to the ground. Four extra balls he had in his pocket fell out, and we ended up with five baseballs on the field.

I picked up the baseball lying nearest me and tagged the runner out. The umpire called him safe, saying he didn't know whether I had the right ball or not.—*David Kalefsky, 16*

I asked Charlie Williams, an umpire in the National League, about your situation, and he told me that very incident occurred while he was umpiring in the minor leagues.

The umpire involved went to his supervisor with the same problem you faced, and the supervisor said the best thing to do immediately after that happens is to call time out. That kills the play.

But that can't be done if the runner has started toward home plate, and the umpire hasn't thought quickly enough to call time out. Then it becomes a judgment call for the umpire.

So the umpire was right in ruling—in his judgment—that you didn't have the right ball. It's strictly up to his judgment.

Who's your favorite baseball player that you would like to model yourself after?—*John Wilson, 14*

The guys who make it to the major leagues and don't have the talent and ability that some of the others have: Players like Pete Rose who don't have all the natural ability but turned into one of the best players ever. That shows me a lot of determination and concentration.

Also, my favorites are those players who are able to go through the

Mickey Mantle, of the great New York Yankee team of the early 1960s. *Below*, display case at the National Baseball Hall of Fame, Cooperstown, New York, showing the evolution of the baseball uniform—*Atlanta Journal & Constitution; Baseball Hall of Fame*

tough times as well as the good. I admire someone like Larry McWilliams who had some excellent years and some trying years, but then bounced back. Through his determination to keep confidence in himself, Larry turned into one of the premier lefthanders in baseball.

Glenn Hubbard is another player who had a chance to make it to the major leagues. It didn't work out, and he was sent back to the minors. But he had the determination to keep working at it.

When people say you can't make it for such and such a reason, you have to show them they're wrong. For instance, I know that Glenn has had people tell him that he wouldn't be able to make it because of his size. He turned into probably the best double-play man in baseball right now.

When I go to major league games, I see people getting drunk. I really hate it, and I hate the things that they say. I don't think it is right for them to sell beer to drunks. I know they are not supposed to, but they do. Do you think they should sell beer to people who are drunk?—*Paige Addicks, 13*

Most problems that arise in the stands are a result of drinking. That's unfortunate because most people go there to enjoy the game. But there are others who go there for other reasons, and they spoil it for most fans.

In Atlanta we have family sections where no alcoholic beverages are served. Other ballparks have done the same, and some teams have gone to selling only low-alcohol beer. After problems with rowdy fans in Detroit, Tiger Stadium instituted a permanent policy of selling only low-alcohol beer.

I admire those teams that are taking a step in the right direction, because you know how I personally feel about alcoholic beverages. I would like to see them not sold anywhere, as far as that is concerned. I know that is not feasible, but I am opposed to drinking alcoholic beverages. However, I am encouraged by the steps some ballparks have taken to make going to the game more enjoyable for those who want to watch the game rather than have to listen to some loud, lewd people who have had too much to drink.

As players we realize that people will cheer for us and people will boo us. I can't say that vulgarity always relates to having too much beer, but I think it's a pretty good guess.

Another thing: People don't realize that they are sometimes sitting next to a player's family.

If you had a choice, what team would you play for?
—Omar Oliver

I would say the 1956 Yankees. But if I had a choice *right now,* I would like to play for a team that has a good chance of going to the

World Series. I wish we had done a lot better this year. It's hard, though, to choose any place but Atlanta as far as the city goes. And I have heard good things about San Diego as well as Toronto.

As far as raising a family and enjoying the lifestyle of the city, it's really hard to beat Atlanta. Other cities that are comparable in those areas are San Diego, Toronto, Cincinnati and Seattle.

But if there were a team that I ever wished to have played for, it would be one of the great Yankees teams when they had Mickey Mantle and Roger Maris and all those other great players. Or playing with Lou Gehrig. What a treat that would have been!

How does a player get into the Hall of Fame?
—*Scot Chernoff, 10*

First of all, the statistics and strength of a player's performance over a career would warrant exceptional status from the voters, the Baseball Writers of America.

A player is eligible only after he has been retired from baseball for five years. To be elected to the Hall of Fame, he must receive 75 percent of the votes. And he has only a certain number of years in which he is eligible. If he hasn't made it to the Hall in that time limit, he can still be selected later by a group of veterans.

People are selected for the Hall of Fame based upon their contributions to baseball—whether as a player, manager, writer, broadcaster or administrator.

A few players have an opportunity to make it to the Hall of Fame their first year of eligibility, and some people won't vote for them just because they don't think it should be unanimous the first time.

The easiest way to make it to the Hall of Fame is to hit 800 home runs or win 300 games as pitcher.

V. Life in the Major Leagues

How do you feel when the Braves are behind at the eighth inning, and then at the ninth you surge ahead and win?— *Sonia Waters, 14*

Baseball is a game of ups and downs. One inning we're completely out of it and the next inning we've won. What's interesting about baseball is that there's no time limit for us to score in the ninth inning. We can keep on scoring until we have won or have made three outs. There's no ten-minute time limit; it may take half an hour.

I've been on the winning—and losing—side in the bottom of the ninth inning. It's a great game and we always have a chance. But sometimes we'll be up and down, up and down. The opposing team could score five runs in the top of the second inning and we could come back and score five in the bottom of the second. All of a sudden we're happy again after things looked so bleak.

It shows the value of having a good, positive attitude throughout the whole game, whether you're ahead 10–0 or behind 10–0. We have to remember that the other team has a chance or that we've got a chance if we're behind. So we have to keep going every inning, every pitch.

What keeps you going in a game that lasts longer than nine innings?— *Melissa Phillips, 17*

Baseball is a unique game in that there is no time limit, and we keep playing until someone wins. Just wanting to win is what keeps us going.

Some of the games definitely do go too long. And some nine-inning games last even longer than extra-inning games. But the players are in pretty good shape to play extra-inning games over the course of the season.

Occasionally, the games do last way into the night, such as the July 4 game in 1985 that lasted until 4 in the morning. And in the minor leagues they have had a 33-inning game.

Often an extra-inning game that is fast-paced is a lot more exciting than a slow-moving, nine-inning contest. It all depends on the excitement level of the game.

Having hit into a double play with the bases loaded and one out, Dale Murphy disgustedly prepares to toss his batting helmet toward the Braves' dugout and head for centerfield—*Rich Addicks, Atlanta Journal & Constitution*

They say you never lose your cool. Is that true?
—Marie Wright, 11

I wish it were true. I make an effort to keep my temper under control although I have been upset with myself before. I've never really gotten upset about an umpire's call, though I've disagreed with him.

Usually I'm upset at myself for not doing what I thought I was capable of doing, and I get a little frustrated out there.

I have found a value in keeping my cool. I'm able to perform better and concentrate on the task at hand if I haven't lost my cool. I've also found that the best philosophy is to never let the other guy know when he's got you frustrated. That gives him the added advantage of saying, "Oh well, look at Murphy over there. He's really mad at himself and I've got him this time. Now I have the edge over him."

I prefer the other team never knowing when I am struggling. If I can always give the feeling that things are going well, that I have confidence, then that gives me the advantage.

Whenever my baseball team loses, it is hard for me to be a good loser. Please tell me how I can learn to be a good loser.— *Justin Zegalia, 10*

The emphasis in amateur athletics has been put so much on winning and losing that the main benefits of athletic competition are sometimes distorted.

In professional athletics, you're paid to perform and perform well, and to win. That's the main goal. In college athletics, the encouragement is there as well, because it does mean a lot of revenue if the program is successful.

What scares me about that philosophy—win at all costs—going any further is that it distorts a participant's feelings at a young age. You're not going to win everything that you take part in. So it's important for you to learn how to take defeat and to learn from it and to improve.

Give your best, honest effort and be satisfied with that. At your young age, you are going to find there will be some victories and some defeats. Just accept both and strive to improve.

Good luck this year. Don't let last year's record affect this year's attitude.

What was your most embarrassing moment in baseball?— *Keron Slaughter, 13*

I've had a number of them. The first that comes to mind is when I was playing Triple-A in Richmond, Virginia, with the Braves farm team, and we were playing the Toledo Mud Hens.

Dale has struck out, the game is over, and he and National League umpire Jim Quick depart for the showers.—*Atlanta Journal & Constitution*

I was the catcher and Roger Alexander was the pitcher. There was a guy on first and Roger threw the ball to me. The guy went to second base and Roger, the pitcher, ducked—as is the custom when the catcher throws to second.

And I hit him—not our second baseman's glove, but Roger, on the hip.

Tommie Aaron was our manager at the time, and Roger had to leave the game.

Roger wasn't too happy about that.

Do you cry when you lose?—*Jennifer Wallace, 9*

There have been times when I've been disappointed, and not because we lost, but because I've been frustrated with myself and kind of depressed after a game. So tears have come to my eyes. But we play 162 games a year. Even if we had a great year and won 100, there would still be 62 losses. So tears don't come after every loss.

I remember I cried in grade school. There was a basketball championship game when I was in the eighth grade. I don't think I had a particularly bad game. It was just an emotional thing, I really wanted to win, and we didn't.

Always keep things in perspective and realize it's a game. The thing you need to remember most is to give 100 percent. That will ease some frustrations.

There are more important things in life to be concerned about than games we play—whether it's you as a youngster or me as an adult. Being upset after a game is natural, but don't let it keep you down.

Does the fans' approval or disapproval of your performance affect your play?—*Michael Strickland, 16*

I try to concentrate on the game and try not to listen to the crowd, although sometimes I've heard some encouraging words—and sometimes some discouraging words. But people clapping and cheering before you come to the plate really helps a player out.

One of the things I like about Atlanta baseball fans is that they are encouraging. Besides Atlanta, I think there are other cities where fans are really behind their team. Los Angeles comes to mind, because their stadium is always packed. Chicago, as well, with Wrigley Field. The bleacher bums there always have a few things to say to players on the visiting team.

But I try not to let it affect me—whether it's approval or disapproval. You can let too much approval go to your head, and you might relax a bit.

Do you ever argue about a bad call?—*Lance Deen, 11*

There have been a lot of times I've talked to the umpire, but I don't really recommend it. I surely don't recommend that you get upset.

But there are times when I question an umpire's call, and I've told him so. For example, if the ball were low I would say, usually on a first-name basis since we're around each other so often, "John (or whatever), don't you think that ball was a little low?" And of course, he says, "I didn't think so or I wouldn't have called it a strike."

I don't think there's anything wrong with occasionally asking the umpire, and sometimes they may say, "Well, I missed that one," or "Maybe you're right. I'll look at it a little closer the next time."

But you have to be careful, because usually when I question the umpire's call I lose my concentration. I'm thinking more about the umpire missing the call than my hitting the next pitch. So it's best to not argue or question the call. If I could do it the way I wanted, I would never question the umpire's call because:

First, you can't change it.

Second, he's just like me—he's going to miss it once in a while. I swing at bad pitches. And they are going to call a ball a strike and sometimes a strike a ball. There's no getting around it. We all make mistakes.

And third, if you get in the habit of being known as a complainer about umpire's calls, that isn't a good reputation to have. Then the umpire loses respect for you.

So it's best not to complain at all.

How do you feel about pitchers deliberately throwing at batters? I just wanted to add that I respect the way you handle yourself on the field. When a fight breaks out, you're always pulling people off each other. I've never seen you throw a punch.—*Stacey Church, 14*

As a hitter, I don't enjoy being thrown at. It's just an unfortunate thing at times that pitchers get a little upset at things and try to retaliate by hitting a batter. It's going to be difficult to stop someone who wants to do that, because it's really hard to tell whether someone does it intentionally or accidentally. A pitcher can disguise it pretty well.

I really look down upon someone who throws deliberately at someone's head. Personally, I don't want anyone throwing at any other part of my body, for that matter. But it happens, and it's something that's tough to eliminate from the game.

Then there are the fights that result sometimes. I usually realize that I have to go out and help my teammates and try to stop the fight if I can. I definitely wouldn't want to go out there and continue the fight with more hitting and stuff like that.

Generally, most of the players out there like to see the fight stopped; just a few are really upset. But we need to be able to keep our emotions in control while we are out there. And it's a challenge to do that, because there is a lot of emotion involved in the game and a lot of nervous energy funneled in the wrong areas.

Why do the opponents shake hands in just about every sport but not after major league baseball games?—*Jadyn Stevens*, 7

That's a good question, and I really don't know the answer. I can only speculate that it's traditional in other sports—hockey and football, for example—that you go by and shake hands. But it's just not a part of the tradition of baseball.

Part of the reason might be that we play 162 games, and often we play the same team three days in a row. It's not as though we have built up ourselves to one showdown of the week where it's such a "battle" and such a physical confrontation. After a boxing match, the fighters embrace; after hockey, it's been so rough you want to shake hands.

In many instances after a big series in baseball, such as the playoffs or World Series, members of one team will go over to the other team's locker room to shake hands. Players and managers will do that, but they won't do it on the field. I think that's the comparison: It was a big, emotional series.

Another factor: The players are not all out on the field at the same time, whereas in football, both teams are out there for the last play of the game. If you're a guard or tackle, the guy you've fought and battled for two or three hours is right there and you can tell him, "Good game." But in baseball the player on your team who makes the last out is usually the only one out there. Since the clubhouse is right behind you, you just turn around and walk into the clubhouse.

I think shaking hands is a good thing in any sport. I don't see anything wrong with it. I think I'd be able to shake the hand of someone who has struck me out. The question is: Would he want to shake my hand after I hit a home run off him?

My dad says you are a religious man. When I play baseball, almost everyone seems to swear and cuss a lot. Is this true in professional baseball, and, if so, how do you handle it? How would you suggest I handle it?—*Allan Farr, 11*

I would suggest that if there is some language that is objectionable to you, then you should try to avoid it if you can. Leave the situation, if it's something that doesn't agree with you. That is what I do.

Basically, I think it is important to give people the opportunity to

An 0-2 pitch sends Dale Murphy ducking against Houston. *Below*, Pascual Perez headed for San Diego's Ed Whitson after being thrown at, whereupon the Padres' bench headed for Perez. The next time up, Perez was thrown at again, and Whitson ejected, but not before a bench-clearing fight.—*Louis Favorite; Rich Addicks, Atlanta Journal & Constitution*

know how you feel, recognize what other people believe, and how they lead their lives. And we need to respect one another's feelings mutually.

Objectionable language is something that I don't enjoy, but I do not try to impose my standards on anyone else. I try to respect them, and I am treated with respect as well.

How do you and the team act when you are under pressure?—*Wesley Clark, 13*

Everyone reacts differently under pressure. Since I have been with the Braves, we have had only a few years where we really had the pressure of a pennant race. Players really are a lot more nervous during the games. There's no question about it.

But any time you go on the field, you want to get a hit, you want to do well and you want to win the game, no matter what position your team has in the standings. Even in spring training—and those games don't mean a thing—when I step into the batter's box I want to get a hit, and I want to win the game.

Sometimes at the end of the season, if the team is not doing well, a player will focus on his personal statistics. That is not very productive and really hurts his performance if he's only concerned about himself. I think it's important to do well to help your team; you can't focus on just yourself.

I think that's one of the values of a pennant race. A player doesn't care what happens when he's right there at the end of the season. He doesn't care how he performs; he just wants to win. If you're out of the pennant race, and you have just no chance, it's really hard not to be too selfish, and you have to guard against that. But if you're in a pennant race, you're a little more nervous about the games. You are under pressure. Your hit, or strikeout, or error stands out more so because it's an important game.

The only thing you can do to deal with pressure is to prepare yourself for the game, give your best, and don't worry about what happens afterward.

Do you have trouble unwinding after a game? Sometimes I can't sleep and I'm just in Little League.—*Billy Taylor, 11*

There are some games that are more exciting than others and they can keep you thinking about them. The best thing I try to remember after a game is over is that it's over.

It's always good to think about the game a little bit and see what you could improve. Maybe there was a mistake you made or something you did right. Think about it and try to remember how you did it.

So after the game is over, think about it a little, then go home and forget it and think about your next game. The worst thing you can do is to let it get to you and interfere with your sleep. That's why it's called a game, because that's all it is. It's important to give your best and win. But win or lose, you can't let it affect your life too much.

After a game, I come home and read a little bit or watch the news and try to relax and think about something else. And it's a little different for us. We play 162 games a year, not a Little League schedule. We also almost *have* to forget the games, or it would drive us crazy. We play almost every night, so we can't dwell on any one game—win or lose.

My main advice to Little Leaguers is to enjoy the game and have fun. It's good to be excited and have butterflies in your stomach. But if you haven't had a good time, it's not worth it.

I play Little League baseball, and when it's the last inning and two outs and a 3–2 count, I am too young for a plug of tobacco to help me concentrate. While I'm in the batter's box, I am very nervous. What would you do in that situation? Is it really true that tobacco settles you down? Most players take tobacco and wrap it around bubble gum. What is that supposed to do?—*Bryant Burns, 12*

First of all, you should never have anything in your mouth during the game—or during any kind of athletic competition (unless it's a mouthpiece for certain contact sports).

I may have a piece of gum or chew on sunflower seeds between innings, but I don't have anything in my mouth while I am out there playing.

Players wrap gum around tobacco to hold it in a ball, and there have been numerous stories about baseball players choking on the tobacco they have been chewing. It's just not worth it if you have to dive for a ball or if you trip and get something lodged in your throat.

Also, it's just not true that tobacco or gum makes you less nervous. That's totally a psychological thing. Sometimes I'm nervous and sometimes I'm relaxed, but what I have in my mouth makes absolutely no difference.

If concentration depended on having something in your mouth, you would see a lot more athletes chewing on things. I think most of them do it out of habit, and with tobacco it's psychologically and physically addictive.

Most important of all, chewing tobacco and dipping snuff endangers your health. Chewing tobacco will cause ugly white patches to form in your mouth and lead to gum deterioration. Many people think "smokeless tobacco" (chewing tobacco and snuff) is harmless. It's not. Last year, a 19-year-old Oklahoma youth died after dipping snuff for six years. He had developed cancer of the mouth that spread throughout his body.

According to the American Cancer Society, 27,000 people in the United States develop oral cancer each year; of that group, more than 9,000 will die. And smokeless tobacco is the major cause.

Sometimes kids think they have to do things like chewing tobacco in order to prove their manliness to their friends. But chewing tobacco has nothing to do with manliness; it's a habit, and a dangerous one.

So you owe it to yourself to forget about tobacco.

With so many pressures in the major leagues, lots of players resort to drugs and alcohol. How do you rid yourself of pressures?—*Andy Lewis, 15*

No matter whether it's professional or high school baseball, at any age—young or old—what helps you perform is your attitude. That goes for any occupation, in or out of the office, as well as any sport.

What helps me is my approach to the game: I work hard, get in shape, do my best and realize that winning and hitting a home run every time out is just not going to happen.

If I give my best effort—100 percent—then success will be there most of the time. I realize that it's impossible to do everything right every time. I won't always make the good catch, the nice throw, or the timely base hit. But I realize that it's not the most important part of my life and I need to work to improve my talents.

Too many people have the incorrect notion that life is always upbeat and expect nothing but smooth sailing. But life is meant to have its challenges. Very few people have succeeded at anything without experiencing failure at some point in their lives. Success is earned, not handed out. And a person needs to deal with both success and failure. That's what life is all about.

One of my favorite sayings is: "It's not the obstacle that's hindering us. It's our inability to cope with it." That's the attitude I try to apply.

There is value to winning. But there also can be value in losing, which can strengthen us for future obstacles. It can make us stronger and teach us to concentrate more on the task at hand, if we have the right frame of mind.

Sure, failure puts pressure on us. But baseball players aren't the only ones who feel it. Doctors and lawyers, businessmen and teachers—anyone who holds a job—will feel pressure to perform. Sometimes

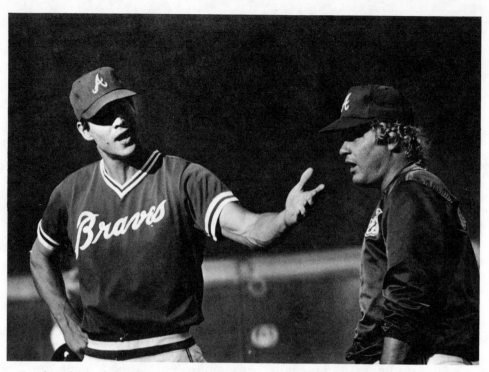

When they're hot, there is no more dreaded one-two punch in major league baseball than the third and fourth hitters in the Atlanta Braves batting order, Dale Murphy and Bob Horner, shown here discussing the metaphysics of the game during a warm-up session.—*Joe Benton, Atlanta Journal & Constitution*

people can't cope and possibly resort to detrimental substances as a crutch to help them through the times they don't succeed.

But there is a lot of pressure in every phase of our lives. That can be good if we use it in a positive way, or we can punish ourselves by resorting to drugs or alcohol. Resorting to those substances basically covers up those times that didn't work out. Using drugs and alcohol doesn't rid yourself of the pressure. They only delay dealing with it.

When we don't measure up to par, and we cloud our minds with drugs and alcohol, we only make the problem worse. And when the pressure is on, we certainly need to think and react clearly. If a person gives in to alcohol or drugs, he may gain a false sense of being in control. Actually, he has submitted himself to more problems with addiction and has surrendered control of his life.

This is what a reformed alcoholic says:

"For an alcoholic, the elevator is going down. He can get off any floor he chooses. The stops include death, jail, insanity, or he can quit."

So nothing but harm comes from drugs and alcohol. The decision has to be made to stay away from these substances.

Pressure exists at all ages, and the earlier you learn to deal with it, the better off you will be. At your age there is probably peer pressure to experiment with these kinds of harmful things.

Life is tough enough without that burden. You can help yourself by eliminating such a problem before it ever starts. Say "no."

Is there anything the other players can do to keep drugs away from sports?—*Tommy Corn, 12*

The main thing a player can do as far as sports is concerned is not to take drugs and show people that you can be successful in your sport and in your life and feel better about yourself for having avoided them.

Whenever someone is involved in an incident with drugs, it just ruins everything in their lives. So you need to try to set an example for your teammates.

My advice to a young player who's talented in baseball:

Don't take that talent for granted, and don't go messing around with drugs and ruin your career—and more important—your life.

Say no. People want you to take drugs so they can take your money. They don't care about your life. And baseball players are open targets for those who prey on people.

Don't get in the situation where you are around people taking drugs.

If you want to be a good athlete, you have to take care of yourself.

And that means no drugs. (And the same thing goes for everyone, really—regardless of your athletic ability.)

With the suspensions of late, I think a majority of players have wised up and have seen that there are big problems if they continue using drugs. Hopefully, we will see a decrease in this problem to the point where baseball is drug-free. That's our goal.

VI. Family and Future Plans

Could you tell me how you and your family handle your "America's hero" status?—*Pam Sisk, 15*

That's really nice of you. I don't feel that way, but that's a nice compliment. I feel fortunate to play baseball, and I'm thankful for the opportunity I have.

I recognize that we—as baseball players—can influence people, especially kids, and I hope that I could use that in a positive way to help others.

You mention my family, and that's the key to my life, and it's important that I keep my priorities in order. I try to keep everything in perspective and just try to make sure that I'm being true to myself.

But maybe what I get from your question, too, is how Nancy and the boys handle the attention. Well, we are still working at it.

Sometimes children of people in the public light get undue pressure and attention. For instance, my oldest boy, Chad, played T-ball. Sometimes there was the expectation by others that Chad should be able to play better than others because I'm his dad. That's attention that Chad shouldn't have had, and it's unfair.

So it will be an interesting challenge for Nancy and me to help Chad and our other boys to realize how to handle the attention of being a baseball player's son.

I will have to teach them that I may have a different occupation than other daddies—but I'm still just a daddy.

How did you and Nancy meet? Was it "love at first sight?"—*Dana Hamilton, 14*

After the 1978 season, I decided I needed to go to college. I went out to Brigham Young University in Utah, and that's where Nancy and I originally met.

When I went out there to school, my friend was Nancy's boyfriend, and that's how we met. Things didn't work out with Nancy and her friend, and we got together and started dating later—in the summer of 1979.

I guess you could say that after we got together and spent some time together, I guess it was love at *third* sight. We were married in October, 1979.

The Messrs. Shawn, Chad, and Travis Murphy, back to camera, inspecting a Halloween pumpkin. *Middle photo*, Dale Murphy supervising a meal for son Shawn, while Travis relaxes nearby. *Below*, Dale and Tyson.

I notice by what I read about you that you have a very close family. What advice can you give me on how to have a close family?—*Tracey Holley, 14*

I think that one thing we try to do is have activities together and enjoy each other's company, play games together, go on picnics, go to ballgames and go to movies as a family.

We try to make sure that we set some time aside each week to be together as a family. With my schedule and Nancy's schedule, we try to make sure that we don't get caught up in our jobs and other things we like to do and neglect the most important part of our lives: our family.

Doing things together, loving one another, doing things for each other are ways to build a close family. Helping one another and showing confidence in one another are important, too. We all have challenges to our lives, and it's important to know that those people who will be right behind us, encouraging us the most, will be our families.

As you and your family grow, you show concern and genuine love for each other, which involves sacrificing for each other. Staying close doesn't mean being close together physically. And as you get older, staying close requires effort.

What's the best Christmas you ever had?—*Kevin Burris, 7*

The one that really sticks out in my mind is the one we had in Nebraska eight or nine years ago.

My parents and my sister and I went back there for Christmas to visit my grandma and my dad's stepfather. My father was born in the tiny town of Cozad. I just remember it because there were so many relatives there, and I can't remember another Christmas where there were that many relatives together.

We had had Christmases with grandmothers and grandfathers, but that time we had a whole slew of people. There were twenty or so relatives in the small town of Brady, not far from North Platte. We were in a small house out in the middle of a farm. It was freezing cold and the atmosphere was so Christmas-like.

Another memorable Christmas was in London in 1978. My parents were living there that year. All I can remember is that it was fun being in Scrooge's country at that time of year.

Christmas four years ago is one of my most memorable. My son Shawn was born on December 17 that year and my oldest son Chad, who was two and a half then, was old enough to know what was going on and be excited about Christmas.

And Christmas season of 1985 was no less memorable: Nancy gave birth to our fourth child, Tyson, a boy.

Thanksgiving, Murphy farm, Brady, Nebraska, 1980. *Below*, Dale and Nancy at about the time of their marriage.

Would you like your boys to play pro baseball like their daddy? What advice would you give them?—*Tuesdi Lorenc, 14*

Actually, I would do like my father did, and just find out what my kids like to do and help them and encourage them to do that. If they want to play baseball, I'll definitely encourage them. There may be other things they want to do, however, and I won't push them into playing baseball.

My advice to them will be: "Find something you like to do, discover what talents you have, and then work as hard as you can to improve yourself and be the best that you can." Then I'll encourage them and give them the opportunity to do it.

The great thing about my parents is that they didn't push me into baseball or sports. I wanted to be involved in it, so they gave me the opportunity and drove me all over for the practices and the games. But I think if I had decided to do something else, they would have helped me pursue that goal just as readily.

Does so much traveling during the season have any effect on the relationship with your family?—*Neil Ruby, 13*

The traveling does have an effect. I don't enjoy traveling that much away from the family. But I'm thankful I don't have to do as much as some other people. In baseball, we have a schedule where we do travel and play games away, but I have friends who are traveling quite a bit more than I do.

I have noticed that when the kids are young, and I go away on a two-week road trip, they seem to change drastically. It really makes me appreciate the time I am with them. Hopefully, after I am through playing baseball, I can get into some kind of profession where I could be with my family.

One of the challenges of being a traveling father and husband is that when I'm on the road, I eat at restaurants all the time. So when I get home, Nancy wouldn't mind going out to eat. But when I get home, the last thing I want to do is go out and get something to eat, because I have been doing that for two weeks. So that's always an interesting challenge.

Also, I've noticed that our phone bills have skyrocketed the past four years because of all the time I've spent on the phone.

Another challenge is sleeping in. On the road you have pretty much your own schedule, but when you come home the kids are usually up a little early. So I have to readjust my schedule, and it's tough.

Do you ever work after the season?—*Mathew Whitney, 8*

Well, yes, but I never get paid for it.

But no, I don't, to be totally honest with you. I don't have a job, really.

Charles and Dale Murphy before tee-off at the "Old Course" at St. Andrews, Scotland, in 1978. *Below*, Nancy, Dale, and Shawn.

There have been some years when I was in the minor leagues where I played a couple of months of winter ball in Florida and one year when I played a few months of winter ball in the Dominican Republic. That's as close as I have been to having a job in the winter.

That's one of the great things about playing professional baseball: You have the opportunity to have some time off. And if you want to seek another career or be involved in some other job, you can do that. Some players I know have worked at television, or local insurance firms and financial management companies in the winter. But what I have tried to do in my situation is take advantage of the time to be with my family. After I'm finished playing baseball, I will not have the free time in the off-season. I will be working year-round.

Right now I have four young boys—Chad, Travis, Shawn, and Tyson—growing up. And I really enjoy the time I have with them.

If you could change anything about yourself, what would it be?—*Laurie Clark, 16*

There are so many things I would like to change I don't know where to begin. A couple of things come to mind:

In baseball, I would like to improve upon my strikeouts, of course. I would like to improve upon my contact and strike out fewer times.

Personally, I feel that I can be more patient. I would like to increase my ability to be patient in all areas of my life—not just in baseball. When things aren't going right on the field, I've learned that it's really helpful to be patient. With my family, I'm not as patient as I could be with my kids, and that's something I need to work on.

Do you think your strong faith in God helps your natural ability on the playing field?—*Stacey Sward, 13*

I think it does. Whatever our occupation is, I think our ability is given to us by the Lord. As we seek His help in all things, He will help us—whether it's our occupation or family or school or anything.

I also think the Lord expects us to do a lot of things on our own. By that I mean I feel that I have been given this talent and ability to play baseball, but I don't think that if I hit a home run or strike out, it's necessarily God's will. Sometimes when I strike out, I have swung at a bad pitch. And sometimes I hit a home run.

Many times I feel I have been blessed by God in my occupation. I don't see any problem in asking for a little help in being able to concentrate in times of need when I may be tired or have problems concentrating that night on the task at hand. And I've said prayers out there on the field.

But just to say that because I didn't hit a home run my prayers weren't answered isn't necessarily true. I think the Lord gives you

The rookie catcher of the Atlanta Braves in September, 1976. The following September, after a season of Triple-A ball at Richmond, he will be back up to stay.

talents and abilities and expects you to put in the extra effort and not always expect a base hit or home run—the results you would have wanted.

Sometimes we get a hit; sometimes we strike out. I think that's our purpose for life: To experience ups and downs and to face the challenges we have. And it's easier to face those challenges with a faith in God, in whom all things are possible.

I would like to know if you have ever thought of playing in the National Basketball Association, because of your height. I feel that you would be another Doctor J.—*Bryant Burns, 10*

I did play basketball in school, but I had quite a bit of foul trouble. I might have been a pretty good basketball player if I had stayed in for the first half. I did get one college offer to play basketball. I think it was the University of Idaho.

I admire Doctor J and what he is able to do on the basketball court. Sometimes I wish I could go out there and do what he does. I think he is one of the greatest athletes of our time, and no one else can do what he can do. I'd never be able to come close. But I would have one thing in common with Doctor J on the basketball court: Big feet.

Is your favorite hobby baseball?—*Amy Kerlin, 9*

When you say "hobby," I usually think of doing something for enjoyment, not for a salary, although I do enjoy playing baseball. If I weren't a professional baseball player, I would probably be playing softball as a hobby.

As far as hobbies are concerned, my favorite is gardening. I'm not very good at it, and I haven't had much experience, but I enjoy planting a garden and seeing things grow. That's my most enjoyable hobby.

My other hobbies include chess, sailing, and ham radio. (I got my novice license for ham radio in December a year ago.)

Do you ever wish you had chosen a career other than major league baseball? If so, what would it have been?
—*Amber McCullough, 13*

There have been a lot of times I wish I had chosen another career. Mostly, when I was in the minor leagues, wondering if I were ever going to make it to the majors. I wondered if the time I was spending in the minors was going to be worth it.

Sometimes, when I didn't do very well, I wondered if I had made the wrong choice or at least whether it was time to make another choice. There were times in the past that I felt like I should have tried something other than being a baseball player.

In 1982 Dale visits with former President Jimmy Carter and his mother, Mrs. Lillian Carter, at Atlanta–Fulton County Stadium.—*Atlanta Braves*

Even now, sometimes it gets a little frustrating when things aren't going very well, and I would wish that I was doing something else rather than trying to hit those curve balls and sliders. But it's a great occupation and I'm happy to be in it. I don't know exactly what I would be doing now. This is the only thing I have really done since I was eight years old.

I have a lot of admiration for doctors. I can't say that I would have the strength to go to school as much as doctors do. But when I think of all the good doctors accomplish for some people, I would love to have been a doctor—using that knowledge to help people.

When you retire, are you planning on being a manager?
—*Amy Warren, 14*

I'm not sure what I'm going to do when I retire, but I do know one thing I am *not* going to do—and that's be a manager.

First of all, with the travel required in baseball, I think I would rather try something different. Also, I really don't have a desire to manage a professional baseball team. I've thought about coaching in amateur athletics, but managing professionally doesn't appeal to me. I think it's got to be inside of you that you've always wanted to manage.

There's no question that the pressure is on a manager, and that there's a big adjustment moving from ballplayer to manager. All of a sudden, everything that goes wrong is your fault. Everyone's mistakes are now your responsibility.

However, the rewards from managing can be great. Molding a successful team is one of the greatest challenges in baseball.

But travel is the biggest roadblock to managing for me. Now if we played all our games here at home, I might think about it. It is a demanding job, and I just don't know if I'm cut out to be a manager. I don't feel like I am right now.

How many more years do you think you can play baseball?—*Rich Diprima, 14*

That's really hard to tell. Right now I'm just trying to make it through this week.

But it really is hard to tell exactly how many years a player can play. You never really do know because injuries can happen. All kinds of things could happen. If a player stays healthy and can continue to produce, he can play until he is close to forty years of age. Those past forty are in a real minority. But not even most players can make it to their mid-thirties.

Since I turned thirty, many people have asked me how much longer I will play, and it's really hard to give a concrete answer right now. There aren't too many occupations that have as much time off as baseball, so that's one thing I'll think about. I could end up changing jobs and be away from home even more.

As I continue to play, I will look at a few factors, including my health, my ability to produce for the team, and my family situation. And when it comes time to step down, I will.

What are you thankful for?—*Stacie Carter, 5*

There is probably not enough room here to say all the things I am thankful for, but:

I'm thankful for my family. I've really enjoyed life since Nancy and I married and had these boys that we have. I'm thankful that we can be together as a family. It gives me a reason to be thankful for everything else.

I'm thankful, too, for my parents who cared for me and loved me and provided all the opportunities for me—not only to play baseball, but also the drum lessons, tennis lessons and golf lessons. They weren't concerned about my becoming a professional musician or athlete; they just cared for me and wanted me to experience those things. But mostly I'm thankful for the love and concern that I received from them.

And as corny as it sounds, I'm thankful, too, for the United States and freedoms we enjoy and the educational opportunities available to my children.

I'm thankful I can do what I want to do. That in itself is something that's taken for granted so much. I'm thankful for the opportunity to play baseball, to perform in a job where I get to work outside in the fresh air most of the time. I get to travel a lot and be involved in something that as a little kid I dreamed a lot about.